≋ fresh and easy ≋
soups
and spectacular
smoothies
for good health

fresh and easy soups and spectacular smoothies for good health

sonia allison

foulsham

LONDON • NEW YORK • TORONTO • SYDNEY

foulsham

The Publishing House, Bennetts Close, Cippenham, Slough, Berkshire, SL1 5AP, England

Foulsham books can be found in all good bookshops or direct from www.foulsham.com

ISBN 13: 978-0-572-03296-8
ISBN 10: 0-572-03296-X

Copyright © 2003 and 2007 W. Foulsham & Co. Ltd

Main cover photograph © Cephas Picture Library
Bottom cover photograph © Anthony Blake Picture Library

A CIP record for this book is available from the British Library

The moral right of the author has been asserted

Previously published as *Real Food Soups and Smoothies from Your Blender*

Printed in Great Britain by Mackays of Chatham plc, Chatham, Kent

CONTENTS

INTRODUCTION

Versatile, healthy, ideal for a quick snack or easy to serve with crusty bread for a main meal, the humble soup comes in so many guises – from a cooling summer-fruit refresher to a thick, spicy and warming winter dish. When I came to put together this new collection, I decided to give it an international flavour to make the most of all the delicious ways of serving soup around the world. Then, of course, I couldn't ignore the soup's cousin – the delicious smoothie. Nourishing, quick and tremendously tasty, they are just right for our hectic modern lifestyle.

Britain has more than her fair share of tomato, mushroom, chicken and oxtail soups and Scotch broth. But head to Holland in the winter and you'll be presented with more yellow pea soup – 'so thick your spoon will stand up in it' – than you'll know what to do with. Further north, in Denmark, Norway and Sweden, many other versions are on offer to the curious.

Finland has adopted from neighbouring Russia its bortsch or beetroot (red beet) soup, along with its own array of soups using every imaginable fish from its unique network of some 60,000 local lakes and rivers. Russia's range of beetroot bortsches includes a glassy clear one in vivid dark red, sometimes served cold. Another group of Russian soups, called shchi, is based on leaves – perhaps cabbage, young nettles, sour-tasting sorrel, spinach or beetroot, or a mixture of greenery depending on the cook's mood. Nearby Poland also specialises in bortsch, which is frequently served with floats of pierogi (which is basically meat-filled ravioli) and traditional chlodnik litewski – white bortsch – which is a gem of a soup heavy with soured (dairy sour) cream, vegetables, cucumber, fresh chives and dill (dill weed), milk and hard-boiled (hard-cooked) eggs. The national summer favourite is sorrel soup, revered for its tangy taste and refreshing qualities. By contrast, in Central Europe, the Czech Republic has its own style of goulash soup (a hangover from the Austro-Hungarian Empire), a hefty onion soup containing dark rye bread, and a sustaining chicken soup with noodles.

Germany goes in for beer soup, a winter breakfast soup with buttermilk, potato soup with or without paprika, and a rugged bean and vegetable soup native to Westphalia. For a touch more elegance, there are clear soups with tiny dumplings and a selection of cream soups. Over to Belgium, whose chervil soup and a soup with green eels strikes an unusual but delicious balance. For the rest of us, the country is renowned for its vegetable purée soups laden with butter and cream. France is closely associated with brown onion soup, vichyssoise and any number of fish soups, headed by Provençal bouillabaisse. Italy is renowned for its lively minestrone, fine consommés with ravioli or tiny pasta, the clear stracciatella (egg lace soup) with eggs and polenta, mussel soup and other fish soups jam-packed with a multitude of locally caught fish. Switzerland stays with comforting cheese soups combined with bread and wine – almost a fondue taste-alike – mixed vegetable soups with rice, and a green onion soup densely packed with snipped fresh chives to give it its emerald colour.

Austria loves dumplings – of whatever size and whether light or heavy – in clear soup and also goes in for stalwarts such as a combo of celeriac (celery root) and potato. There is also goulash soup full of meat or poultry and mild red paprika, bread soup and garlic soup amid a vast repertoire of other hot and cold specialities, with thoughtful seasoning and always tastefully presented. Hungary's great classic, apart from goulash soup, is halaszle, a soup packed with choice local fish such as carp, pike, perch and kecsege (a fish related to the sturgeon), and seasoned mightily with paprika and onion.

Bulgaria specialises in hot and cold yoghurt soups while Romania has fanciful mixes of beef soup beaten with eggs, vegetable soups with ham and noodles, and a vast haricot (navy) bean soup – again called bortsch – with a cornucopia of vegetables including raw beetroot (red beet). Yugoslavia's most important soups are those based on fish, while Turkey has a rich and golden red lentil soup, another with tripe and something called wedding soup, a celebratory affair filled to the brim with meat, mixed vegetables, eggs and lemon. Greece is conservative where soup is concerned and her best known one is avogolemono, a lightish and mild chicken soup containing rice, eggs and lemon juice. But look hard and you'll probably be able to track down kakavia, which is similar to bouillabaisse, and other appetising soups based on chick peas (garbanzos), lentils and beans. Spain is renowned for chilled gazpachos, red ones with tomatoes and white ones with almonds and milk. Hot soups appear with fish and eggs. Portugal's national soup is caldo verde, or green cabbage, but she also has an engaging tomato soup and innumerable others using local meat, fish, seasonal vegetables, sausages, bacon, ham and spices such as cinnamon.

North Africa goes in for lentil soup, as does Turkey, along with throat-grabbing vegetable soups laced with spice and fire and dancing with chick peas and chillies. Examples are Algeria's chorba hamra and Morocco's harira, stuffed to the gunwales with fresh and dried vegetables, pasta and lamb and eaten to break the fast during the holy month of Ramadam. Even the rest of sun-baked Africa has a collection of soups that use local ingredients like okra (ladies' fingers), black-eyed beans and other dried pulses, squashes, yams, sweet potatoes, plantains, tomatoes, onions, garlic, seafood, peanuts, tapioca and sparing amounts of meat.

The Americas, Australia and New Zealand borrow much from Europe and the Far East and cleverly and convincingly adapt concepts and recipes to suit seasonal ingredients, climate and national tastes, producing a brilliant band of homespun classic soups or the now fashionable fusion, a combination of East and West.

Asia, from Thailand to China to Japan, has at least as many soups as everywhere else put together. India alone appears to be a non-soup-drinking nation unless you count dahl, a 'stew' of lentils and spices, usually eaten there as a meal with rice but thinned down to a liquid elsewhere and served as soup in Anglo-Indian restaurants. I doubt its authenticity.

This book offers more than a hundred innovative and easily made recipes, featuring both familiar tastes and foreign flavours. The rest of the world is never far away from our soup bowls.

SOUPS AND SMOOTHIES STORECUPBOARD

It is useful to carry a comprehensive range of ingredients at home in case you suddenly decide to make a soup or smoothie but have no time for shopping. Under each of the following headings you will find a list of useful items to keep on hand should the need arise. Apart from the usual storecupboard staples like flour and rice, salt and pepper, mustard and vinegars, there are many additions that take into account the recipes in this book.

Dry stores and packets
- Rice: fragrant Thai, brown or white basmati, brown rice flakes, imperial red
- Nuts: macadamia, almonds including flaked (slivered), pine nuts, pistachios, walnuts
- Pasta: rice noodles, quick-cook macaroni
- Grains and pulses: tapioca, barley, porridge oats, couscous, puy lentils, orange lentils, yellow split peas, butter (lima) beans
- Gelatine
- Stock (bouillon) powder or cubes: fish, chicken, beef, vegetable
- Sugar: white and brown
- Dried fruits: sultanas (golden raisins), raisins, apricots
- Flours: plain (all-purpose), potato flour (farina), cornflour (cornstarch)
- Seasonings: white and black pepper, salt

Canned and bottled foods
- Fish sauce
- Coconut milk
- Oils: olive, sunflower, sesame, groundnut (peanut)
- Alcohol: red, rosé and white wines, Campari, amaretto di saronno, apricot brandy, orange-flavoured liqueur, crème de cassis, crème de menthe, sparkling perry, sweet cider, medium sherry, Pernod or Ricard

- Fruit juices: passion, tropical, orange, apple, pineapple, peach, mango, custard apple, pink grapefruit, cranberry, sparkling red and white grape juice, tomato, carrot
- Cold drinks: lemonade, orangeade, dry ginger ale
- Crunchy peanut butter
- Beef consommé
- Pulses: red kidney beans, chick peas (garbanzos), mushy peas
- Preserves: orange marmalade, clear honey, set honey, caramel-flavoured syrup
- Vegetables: artichoke hearts, pimientos, tomatoes
- Tuna in brine
- Fruit: mandarin oranges, fruit cocktail, grapefruit segments, pears, assorted fruit fillings
- Pickled beetroot (red beet)

Herbs, flavourings and condiments

- Spices: mild curry powder, Madras curry powder, turmeric, saffron, tandoori spice mix, chilli powder, cinnamon, bay leaves, five-spice powder, garam masala, ground cumin, ground coriander (cilantro), ground cardamom, whole and ground allspice, mustard powder, nutmeg
- Cordials: ginger and lemon grass, elderflower, grenadine syrup
- Herbs: tarragon, thyme, sage, basil
- Flower waters: rose and orange
- Flavourings: anchovy essence (extract), mushroom ketchup (catsup), soy sauce, chilli sauce, Worcestershire sauce, Tabasco sauce (green and red), Angostura bitters, brown ketchup, creamed horseradish, English mustard, wholegrain mustard, Dijon mustard, juniper berries, pesto, mango chutney, redcurrant jelly (clear conserve), tahini, capers
- Vinegars: cider, sherry, malt, chilli, balsamic
- Dried vegetables: red chillies, sun-dried tomatoes, porcini mushrooms
- Purées (pastes): tomato, sun-dried tomato, chilli

Chilled foods

- Cheeses: Cheddar, Stilton, Parmesan, Mascarpone, Mozzarella, Feta
- Dairy: buttermilk, crème fraîche, soured (dairy sour) cream, full cream milk, skimmed milk, plain yoghurt, butter, custard sauce
- Herbs: red and green fresh chillies, fresh root ginger, garlic
- Juices: fresh lemon and lime
- Fruits: lemons, limes
- White bread

Frozen foods

- Prawns (shrimp)
- Lemon grass stalks
- Lime leaves
- Vanilla ice cream
- Sorbets
- Chestnuts
- Peas

NOTES ON THE RECIPES

- Do not mix metric, imperial and American measures. Follow one set only.
- All spoon measures are level unless otherwise stated:
  1 tsp = 5 ml; 1 tbsp = 15 ml.
- Eggs are medium.
- Thoroughly wash all vegetables and fruit before use and, to remove pesticides from citrus fruit skins, scrub well with a brush under running water. Scrub, scrape or peel vegetables as appropriate.
- Fish, poultry and meat should be rinsed before using in recipes and cooked and raw items must be kept well apart to prevent contamination and possible food poisoning.
- Fresh and frozen herbs have the most authentic flavours but, if unavailable, use half the quantity given of dried. There is no substitute for fresh parsley, coriander (cilantro) and dill (dill weed).
- Always use the oil specified in the recipe.
- Margarine may be substituted for butter, but check the packet to ensure it is suitable for the particular use.
- Preparation and cooking times are approximate.
- Use labour-saving kitchen appliances for speed such as a food processor for slicing, chopping and grinding. A mandolin also works well.
- You can adjust the texture of soups by blending coarsely or finely, or by leaving some or all of the ingredients simply chopped.
- When adding crème fraîche to soup, do not allow it to boil. The soup may be brought just up to boiling point, then quickly taken away from the heat.
- It is better for your health to reduce your overall salt intake. Season soups with herbs and pepper to taste, bearing in mind that flavours intensify after the soup has been made, then taste and add a little salt if you wish. You may find that chilled soups need more generous seasoning than hot soups.

CHILLED SAVOURY SOUPS

Savoury chilled soups, based mostly on vegetable combinations, are perfect for the summer months and make cooling and innovative meal starters for any occasion. The best-known favourites are gazpacho and vichyssoise, but just as refreshing are soups made from cucumber, tomatoes, mushrooms, avocados, watercress, peppers, spinach, beetroot (red beet) and peas. Some of the soups in this section have foreign overtones but most of them use familiar and popular ingredients that are easily found in local food stores.

You may find that chilled soups need a little more seasoning than hot soups. Experiment until you get it right and use additional herbs rather than adding too much salt.

A lightly spiced flavour of the exotic with a twist – the soup is poured over ice cubes to give it a cooling effect making this gentle-tasting soup a fabulous summer starter. Serve it before a barbecue or a selection of cold meats.

middle eastern tahini soup with chick peas and lemon

SERVES 6–8

450 ml/¾ pt/2 cups tahini
600 ml/1 pt/2½ cups vegetable
  stock or water
Juice of 3 large lemons
2 garlic cloves, crushed
15 ml/1 tbsp finely chopped fresh
  mint

A pinch of salt and freshly ground
  black pepper
Ice cubes
100 g/4 oz/⅔ cup canned chick peas
  (garbanzos), rinsed and drained
A few sprigs of fresh parsley

1 Blend together the tahini, stock or water, lemon juice and garlic.

2 Stir in the mint and season to taste with salt and pepper.

3 Pour into bowls over ice cubes.

4 Divide the chick peas between the bowls, add a few parsley sprigs to each one and serve.

PREPARATION TIME: 10 MINUTES

A summer soup with a kick! This is a sharply sweet-sour soup combining pickled cucumbers with soured cream and Pernod. The soup is chilled before serving and provides a refreshing respite from the heat of summer.

sour cucumber soup with pernod

SERVES 4

350 g/12 oz/5 cups pickled sweet-sour (dill) cucumbers, diced
225 g/8 oz/1 cup unpeeled fresh cucumber, coarsely chopped
150 ml/¼ pt/⅔ cup sweet-sour cucumber water

300 ml/½ pt/1¼ cups cold water
45 ml/3 tbsp Pernod or Ricard
2 garlic cloves, crushed
Salt and freshly ground black pepper
90 ml/6 tbsp soured (dairy sour) cream or crème fraîche

1 Blend the pickled and fresh cucumbers, cucumber water and cold water in two batches until very smooth. Pour into a bowl.

2 Add the Pernod or Ricard with the garlic and season to taste with salt and pepper.

3 Cover and chill thoroughly.

4 Before serving, stir the soup well, pour into bowls and top each one with a generous dollop of the soured cream or crème fraîche.

PREPARATION TIME: 15 MINUTES

An attractive addition to the summer table, this soup has a lovely green colour and tastes fabulous. For a tasty main meal, serve with warmed crusty bread. If preferred, omit the pepper strips and sprinkle the soup with croûtons.

cucumber soup with garlic and green pepper ribbons

SERVES 4

1 medium cucumber, peeled and cubed
60 ml/4 tbsp chopped fresh dill (dill weed)
2 garlic cloves, peeled

Salt and freshly ground black pepper
450 ml/¾ pt/2 cups low-fat set yoghurt
1 small green (bell) pepper, seeded and cut into fine strips

1 Place the cucumber, dill and garlic in the blender and add half the yoghurt. Blend until smooth, then transfer to a bowl and season to taste with salt and pepper.

2 Gently whisk in the remaining yoghurt.

3 Cover the bowl, then chill the soup thoroughly.

4 Before serving, stir the soup, pour into bowls and sprinkle each portion with the pepper strips.

PREPARATION TIME: 15 MINUTES

bulgarian yoghurt and cucumber soup with walnuts

SERVES 4

1 Prepare as for Cucumber Soup with Garlic and Green Pepper Ribbons, but add 50 g/2 oz/½ cup of chopped walnuts with the dill and omit the pepper strips.

This is a tasty and nutritious soup. The delicious addition of orange-flavoured liqueur brings some colourful flavour to this wonderfully delicate dish, perfect for a sultry evening. Ring the changes by using sweet potato for some extra flavour.

chilled carrot and potato soup with orange liqueur

SERVES 8

700 g/1½ lb carrots, cut into large
  cubes
700 g/1½ lb potatoes, cut into large
  cubes
2 onions, sliced
1.5 litres/2½ pts/6 cups water

5 ml/1 tsp salt
60 ml/4 tbsp orange-flavoured
  liqueur
150 ml/¼ pt/⅔ cup crème fraîche
45 ml/3 tbsp chopped fresh dill
  (dill weed)

1 Place the carrots, potatoes and onions in a large saucepan with the water and salt. Bring to the boil.

2 Lower the heat, cover and simmer for 20–30 minutes or until the vegetables are soft.

3 Remove from the heat and leave to cool. Do not drain.

4 When lukewarm, blend in two or three batches until smooth.

5 Transfer to a large bowl, cover and leave to cool completely, then chill for several hours.

6 Before serving, gently whisk in the liqueur and crème fraîche. Sprinkle each portion with the dill.

PREPARATION TIME: 30 MINUTES
COOKING TIME: 30–40 MINUTES

A truly Mexican-style soup packed with vitamins, the mild flavour of the kidney beans and avocadoes are given a boost with a dash of Tabasco sauce. It makes a substantial meal in itself, especially if served with tortilla chips for dipping.

guacamole soup
with red kidney beans

SERVES 6

400 g/14 oz/1 large can of red
  kidney beans, rinsed and drained
6 spring onions (scallions), sliced
2 ripe avocados, halved and stoned
  (pitted)
1 green chilli, halved and seeded
30 ml/2 tbsp tomato purée (paste)
Juice of 2 limes

5 ml/1 tsp salt
5 ml/1 tsp Tabasco sauce
600 ml/1 pt/2½ cups vegetable
  stock
30 ml/2 tbsp cider vinegar

TO SERVE:
Tortilla chips

1   Blend the contents of the can of kidney beans to a coarse purée.

2   Add the remaining ingredients except half the stock and the vinegar and blend briefly until just chopped.

3   Transfer to a large bowl and slowly whisk in the remaining stock.

4   Stir in the cider vinegar, then cover the bowl and chill for several hours until very cold.

5   Stir well before serving with tortilla chips, if desired.

PREPARATION TIME: 25 MINUTES

This is an unusual but delightful soup that combines watercress with elderflower cordial. It is soothing and elegant and is light enough to enjoy either for lunch or as a starter. Perfect to serve when entertaining outdoors during the summer months.

watercress, onion and celery soup with elderflower

SERVES 4–6

150 g/5 oz watercress
2 onions, cut into chunks
3 celery sticks, thinly sliced
450 ml/¾ pt/2 cups full cream milk

450 ml/¾ pt/2 cups water
5 ml/1 tsp salt
30 ml/2 tbsp elderflower cordial

1 Place all the ingredients except the elderflower cordial in a saucepan and bring to the boil, stirring.

2 Lower the heat, cover and simmer for 30 minutes, stirring occasionally, until the vegetables are soft.

3 Remove from the heat and leave to cool. Do not drain.

4 When lukewarm, blend in two or three batches until just smooth.

5 Transfer to a large bowl and stir in the elderflower cordial. Cover and chill.

6 Stir well before serving.

PREPARATION TIME: 15 MINUTES

COOKING TIME: 30 MINUTES

A mild flavoured soup that incorporates some of the best English ingredients on offer. The watercress provides a wonderfully peppery taste that complements the leek and potatoes perfectly. Serve with a selection of breads for a delicious meal.

watercress and leek thick cream soup

SERVES 6

1 large leek, halved lengthways and coarsely chopped
100 g/4 oz watercress
350 g/12 oz potatoes, peeled and diced

900 ml/1½ pts/3¾ cups water
150 ml/¼ pt/⅔ cup full cream milk
5 ml/1 tsp salt
150 ml/¼ pt/⅔ cup single (light) cream

1 Place all the ingredients except the cream in a large saucepan and bring to the boil.

2 Lower the heat, cover and simmer for 25 minutes or until the vegetables are very soft.

3 Remove from the heat and leave to cool completely. Do not drain.

4 Blend in two or three batches until smooth.

5 Transfer to a large bowl, cover and chill for several hours.

6 Stir in the cream before serving.

PREPARATION TIME: 15 MINUTES
COOKING TIME: 30 MINUTES

The mildly flavoured pimientos, yoghurt and mascarpone are given a kick-start by the addition of chilli powder. To make the most of the slightly sweet-sour flavours, eat the soup within 24-hours of making it.

pimiento soup with yoghurt, mascarpone and chilli

SERVES 6

400 g/14 oz/1 large can of whole pimientos in brine, rinsed and drained
125 g/4½ oz/generous ½ cup Mascarpone cheese
200 ml/7 fl oz/scant 1 cup plain yoghurt
350 ml/12 fl oz/1⅓ cups water

2.5–5 ml/½–1 tsp chilli powder
200 ml/7 fl oz/scant 1 cup tomato juice
30 ml/2 tbsp sherry vinegar

TO SERVE:
Grated orange rind (optional)

1 Tip the contents of the can of pimientos into the blender. Add the Mascarpone, yoghurt, water and chilli powder and blend until very smooth.

2 Transfer to a bowl, add the tomato juice and vinegar and stir well. Cover and chill for several hours.

3 Stir well before serving sprinkled with a little grated orange rind, if liked.

PREPARATION TIME: 10 MINUTES

Spinach is packed full with vitamins and minerals including vitamin C, iron, calcium, and potassium. Baby spinach is a tender and mild-flavoured green and in this recipe the mildness of the flavour is given a lift by the herbed cheese.

spinach and herbed cream cheese soup

SERVES 4–6

175 g/6 oz fresh baby leaf spinach
600 ml/1 pt/2½ cups vegetable
    stock
450 ml/¾ pt/2 cups skimmed milk

150 g/5 oz/⅔ cup full fat cream
    cheese with fines herbes
Salt and freshly ground black pepper

1   Place the spinach, stock and milk in a large saucepan and bring to the boil.

2   Lower the heat, cover and simmer for 10 minutes.

3   Remove from the heat and leave to cool completely. Do not drain.

4   Add the cheese and blend in two or three batches until smooth.

5   Pour into a large bowl and season to taste with salt and pepper. Cover and chill for several hours.

6   Stir thoroughly before serving.

PREPARATION TIME: 10 MINUTES
COOKING TIME: 10 MINUTES

This Far Eastern inspired recipe looks highly attractive on the table when served sprinkled with colourful grated orange rind. There are many different types of mushroom now available in supermarkets so try experimenting with the different flavours.

oriental mushroom and rice milk soup

SERVES 6

500 g/18 oz mushrooms, coarsely chopped
30 ml/2 tbsp toasted sesame oil
900 ml/1½ pts/3¾ cups unflavoured rice milk
1 garlic clove, crushed

15–20 ml/1–1½ tbsp soy sauce
10 ml/2 tsp cornflour (cornstarch)
300 ml/½ pt/1¼ cups water
45 ml/3 tbsp snipped fresh chives
15 ml/1 tbsp grated orange rind

1   Fry the mushrooms in the sesame oil in a large saucepan until tender.

2   Mix in 600 ml/1 pt/2½ cups of the rice milk, the garlic and soy sauce and bring to the boil, stirring.

3   Lower the heat, cover and simmer gently for 15 minutes.

4   Mix the cornflour to a smooth paste with a little of the remaining rice milk. Mix in the rest of the milk and the water, then pour into the saucepan.

5   Bring gently to the boil, stirring, then lower the heat and simmer for 2 minutes, stirring, until thickened.

6   Remove from the heat and leave to cool completely.

7   If you want a smooth soup, blend in two or three batches until smooth, then transfer to a large bowl. Cover and chill for several hours.

8   Stir before serving, sprinkling each portion with the chives and orange rind.

PREPARATION TIME: 15 MINUTES
COOKING TIME: 25 MINUTES

Garlic is well known for helping to reduce high blood pressure and cholesterol, while Walnuts are packed with linolenic acid that converts easily to heart-healthy omega-3 fatty acids. If you prefer, you can add the nuts before blending.

chestnut mushroom soup
with garlic and fried walnuts

SERVES 4

225 g/8 oz chestnut mushrooms, broken into pieces
4 garlic cloves, peeled and halved
300 ml/½ pt/1¼ cups milk
7.5 ml/1½ tsp salt
5 ml/1 tsp dried thyme

7.5 ml/1½ tsp ground cumin
300 ml/½ pt/1¼ cups water
15 g/½ oz/1 tbsp butter
5 ml/1 tsp olive oil
50 g/2 oz/½ cup shelled walnuts, coarsely chopped

1   Place the mushrooms and garlic in a pan with the milk, salt, thyme, cumin and water.

2   Bring to the boil, then lower the heat, cover and simmer for 15 minutes.

3   Meanwhile, heat the butter gently in a separate pan with the oil until melted. Add the walnuts and fry (sauté) over a medium-low heat for 5 minutes.

4   Allow the soup to cool to lukewarm.

5   Blend in two or three batches to a coarse purée, transfer to a large bowl, stir in the nuts, cover and chill for several hours.

6   Stir well before serving.

PREPARATION TIME: 20 MINUTES
COOKING TIME: 20 MINUTES

This is a simple yet delicious soup that has a wonderfully zippy tang and vibrant colour. Trying ringing the changes by experimenting with different herbs, such as coriander, or using fresh tomatoes and carrots if you have the time.

tomato and carrot soup with basil and mint

SERVES 4

400 g/14 oz/1 large can of tomatoes
400 g/14 oz/1 large can of sliced
   carrots in water
6 fresh basil leaves
6 fresh mint leaves

5 ml/1 tsp caster (superfine) sugar
15 ml/1 tbsp brown sauce
300 ml/½ pt/1¼ cups chilled water
Salt and freshly ground black pepper

1   Tip the contents of the cans of tomatoes and carrots into the blender.

2   Add the remaining ingredients except the salt and pepper and blend until smooth.

3   Pour into a bowl, cover and chill thoroughly for several hours.

4   Stir and season to taste with salt and pepper before serving.

PREPARATION TIME: 10 MINUTES

Beetroot is traditionally a winter vegetable but can be obtained year round in most good supermarkets. When fresh, its nutty flavour complements the horseradish perfectly. Don't even be tempted to use pickled beetroot from a jar for this recipe!

beetroot soup with tomatoes and horseradish

SERVES 8

450 g/1 lb ripe tomatoes, blanched, skinned and quartered
700 g/1½ lb cooked beetroot (red beet), peeled and cut into chunks
2 garlic cloves, peeled and halved
30 ml/2 tbsp creamed horseradish
750 ml/1¼ pt/3 cups water
30 ml/2 tbsp cider vinegar
Salt and freshly ground black pepper
60 ml/4 tbsp crème fraîche

1 Blend the tomatoes, beetroot and garlic in two batches until smooth.

2 Transfer to a bowl and gently whisk in the horseradish, water and vinegar.

3 Cover and chill for several hours until very cold.

4 Stir well and season with salt and pepper to taste before serving, topping each portion with a swirl of the crème fraîche.

PREPARATION TIME: 20 MINUTES

A soup for all you slimmers out there! This is a deliciously refreshing soup that is very low in fat. The use of buttermilk ensures that you get a lovely creamy texture and taste that helps to soften the slight acidity of the fresh lemon juice.

beetroot and lemon soup with buttermilk

SERVES 4

450 g/1 lb cooked beetroot (red beet), peeled and cubed
450 ml/¾ pt/2 cups water
Juice of 1 large lemon

1 garlic clove, sliced
5 ml/1 tsp garlic salt
250 ml/8 fl oz/1 cup buttermilk

1 Blend all the ingredients except the buttermilk until very smooth.

2 Transfer to a bowl and gently whisk in the buttermilk. Cover and chill for several hours.

3 Stir before serving.

PREPARATION TIME: 10 MINUTES

This elegant soup is perfect for using as an appetiser when entertaining as it can be made well in advance and kept chilled until required. Try to use tomatoes that are in season as this will ensure your soup will taste sun-ripened, sweet and delicious.

fresh tomato consommé with sherry

SERVES 6

20 ml/4 tsp powdered gelatine	5 ml/1 tsp green Tabasco sauce
30 ml/2 tbsp cold water	10 ml/2 tsp Worcestershire sauce
30 ml/2 tbsp hot water	30 ml/2 tbsp medium-dry sherry
700 g/1½ lb tomatoes, skinned and quartered	Freshly ground black pepper
	20 ml/4 tsp snipped fresh chives

1 Place the gelatine in a saucepan. Add the cold water and leave to soften for 5 minutes. Stir in the hot water, then melt over the lowest possible heat until clear.

2 Place the tomatoes, Tabasco and Worcestershire sauces and sherry in the blender and blend until smooth.

3 Transfer to a bowl and stir in the warm melted gelatine. Cover and chill until softly set and really cold.

4 Break up with a spoon, season to taste with pepper and serve with a sprinkling of the chives on each portion.

PREPARATION TIME: 20 MINUTES

The quintessential chilled soup! Originating in hot and sunny Spain, this cooling soup can't be beaten when the temperatures rise and you want something delicious to eat. Serve with any of the accompaniments listed below.

gazpacho

SERVES 6

450 g/1 lb ripe tomatoes, blanched, skinned and coarsely sliced

1–2 garlic cloves, peeled and each cut into 3

1 red (bell) pepper, halved, seeded and cut into strips

1 green pepper, halved, seeded and cut into strips

1 onion, chopped

½ unpeeled cucumber, diced

45 ml/3 tbsp tomato purée (paste)

10 ml/2 tsp caster (superfine) sugar

45 ml/3 tbsp olive oil

30 ml/2 tbsp sherry vinegar

2 large slices of white bread, crumbed

300 ml/½ pt/1¼ cups water

OPTIONAL ACCOMPANIMENTS:

Coarsely chopped cucumber, diced red and green peppers, chopped hard-boiled (hard-cooked) egg, coarsely chopped red onion, croûtons

1 Place the tomatoes, garlic, pepper strips, onion, cucumber, tomato purée and sugar in a large bowl and mix together.

2 Blend in two batches until smooth, then return to the bowl.

3 Whisk in the olive oil and vinegar, then gently mix in the breadcrumbs and water.

4 Cover and chill for several hours until very cold.

5 Stir before serving with dishes of your chosen additions served separately.

PREPARATION TIME: 20–25 MINUTES

(LONGER IF ADDITIONS ARE INCLUDED)

This classic soup is actually American in origin, being first created at the Ritz-Carlton Hotel in New York by a French chef called Louis Diat in 1917. Its enduring popularity is probably due to its delicious mild and creamy flavour.

vichyssoise

SERVES 6

4 young leeks
1 onion, peeled and sliced
450 g/1 lb potatoes, peeled and
  cubed
1 litre/1¾ pts/4¼ cups water

5 ml/1 tsp salt
300 ml/½ pt/1¼ cups whipping
  cream
60 ml/4 tbsp snipped fresh chives

1 Discard most of the green part from the leeks. Slit the remaining white parts lengthways and wash thoroughly between the leaves. Slice.

2 Place in a large saucepan with the onion, potatoes, water and salt and bring gently to the boil.

3 Lower the heat, cover and simmer gently for 50–60 minutes or until the vegetables are very soft.

4 Leave to cool to lukewarm, then blend in two or three batches until very smooth.

5 Transfer to a large bowl and gently whisk in the cream. Cover and chill for several hours.

6 Stir before serving sprinkled with the chives.

PREPARATION TIME: 20 MINUTES
COOKING TIME: 1¼ HOURS

Peas are an excellent source of protein and so even though this soup only has four ingredients, it is flavoursome, colourful and nutritious. If you are not keen on mushy peas, you can substitute them with marrowfat peas instead.

creamy pea soup with fresh mint

SERVES 4

400 g/14 oz/1 large can of mushy
   peas
5 ml/1 tsp chopped fresh mint
600 ml/1 pt/2½ cups vegetable
   stock

60 ml/4 tbsp whipping cream
Thinly sliced fresh mint leaves, to
   garnish

1 Blend the peas, chopped mint and stock until smooth.

2 Transfer to a saucepan, stir in the cream and heat gently, without boiling, until well blended.

3 Leave to cool to lukewarm, then cover and chill.

4 Stir before serving, sprinkled with the sliced mint.

PREPARATION TIME: 5 MINUTES
COOKING TIME: 5 MINUTES

Lettuce may not be an obvious choice of ingredient for a soup but if you use fully grown summer lettuces they have a distinctive, tasty flavour. With so many varieties available now, you can experiment as often as you like with this recipe.

lettuce, garlic and feta cheese soup

SERVES 6

3 round lettuces, finely shredded
3 garlic cloves, halved
1 litre/1¾ pts/4¼ cups water
10 ml/2 tsp caster (superfine) sugar
5 ml/1 tsp salt

30 ml/2 tbsp potato flour (farina)
150 ml/¼ pt/⅔ cup milk
200 g/7 oz/1¾ cups Feta cheese, crumbled
Chopped fresh mint, to garnish

1 Place the lettuce in a saucepan with the garlic, water, sugar and salt. Cook gently over a low heat until wilted.

2 Mix the potato flour to a smooth paste with a little of the milk. Add the remaining milk and stir into the pan.

3 Bring to the boil, stirring all the time. Lower the heat, cover and simmer for 20 minutes.

4 Allow the soup to cool almost completely.

5 Blend in two batches until smooth, then transfer to a bowl, stir in the Feta, cover and chill.

6 Stir before serving sprinkled with a little chopped mint.

PREPARATION TIME: 20 MINUTES
COOKING TIME: 25 MINUTES

CHILLED SWEET SOUPS

The foundation of most of these soups is fruit and I have taken you through the seasons with rhubarb for late spring, berries for summer, currants for autumn (fall) and cranberries for winter. Other soups in this chapter are made using apples, oranges, apricots, pears and melon. Most of these are smooth, blended soups.

This unusual soup makes the most of the spring fruits traditional English country gardens have to offer. The tartness of the fruit is mellowed by the addition of cream which makes for a delicious soup that would be perfect for a dinner party.

gooseberry and rhubarb country garden soup

SERVES 6

225 g/8 oz gooseberries, topped and tailed
175 g/6 oz rhubarb sticks, chopped
600 ml/1 pt/2½ cups water
225 g/8 oz/1 cup caster (superfine) sugar

15 ml/1 tbsp cornflour (cornstarch)
150 ml/¼ pt/⅔ cup apple juice
150 ml/¼ pt/⅔ cup single (light) cream
30 ml/2 tbsp chopped walnuts

1 Place the gooseberries and rhubarb in a saucepan with the water. Bring to the boil.

2 Lower the heat, cover and simmer gently for 20 minutes.

3 Add the sugar and stir until dissolved. Remove from the heat and leave to cool to lukewarm.

4 Blend in two or three batches until just smooth, then transfer to a clean saucepan.

5 Mix the cornflour to a smooth paste with the apple juice. Add to the soup, then gently bring to the boil and simmer for 1 minute until the soup is slightly thickened.

6 Pour into a bowl and place a round of damp greaseproof (waxed) paper directly on top of the soup.

7 Leave to cool, then chill for several hours until very cold.

8 Before serving, remove the greaseproof paper (any layer of skin will come away with it), stir round and pour into six bowls. Drizzle the cream over each portion and sprinkle with the walnuts.

PREPARATION TIME: 20 MINUTES
COOKING TIME: 25 MINUTES

This is a perfect midsummer treat using delicious soft fruits. Try and use fruits that are in season as the end result will be sweeter, fruitier and full of flavour. Needless to say, the soup complements the rest of the rosé wine perfectly!

strawberry and raspberry rosé soup

SERVES 6

450 g/1 lb strawberries, hulled
225 g/8 oz raspberries
900 ml/1½ pts/3¾ cups water
1½ large slices of white bread, cubed
150 g/5 oz/⅔ cup caster (superfine) sugar

1 wine glass rosé wine
10 ml/2 tsp cornflour (cornstarch)
15 ml/1 tbsp lemon juice
150 ml/¼ pt/⅔ cup single (light) cream

1 Place the strawberries and raspberries in a saucepan with the water and bread. Bring gently to the boil.

2 Lower the heat, part-cover and simmer gently for 30 minutes, stirring from time to time.

3 Mix in the sugar and wine and allow cool to lukewarm.

4 Blend in two or three batches until smooth, then transfer to a clean saucepan.

5 Mix the cornflour to a smooth paste with the lemon juice. Add to the soup and bring gently to the boil. Lower the heat and simmer for 2 minutes.

6 Place a round of damp greaseproof (waxed) paper directly on top of the soup. Leave to cool, then chill for several hours until very cold.

7 Before serving, remove the greaseproof paper (any layer of skin will come away with it), stir round and pour into six bowls. Drizzle the cream over each portion.

PREPARATION TIME: 15 MINUTES

COOKING TIME: 35–40 MINUTES

A full-flavoured soup based on two firm favourites: redcurrants and blackcurrants. Crème de cassis (blackcurrant liqueur) strengthens the flavours but for a cheaper alternative, try using a good quality rich blackcurrant juice.

currant soup
with crème de cassis

SERVES 4

350 g/12 oz fresh red or blackcurrants or a mixture of both
600 ml/1 pt/2½ cups water
15 ml/1 tbsp grated lemon rind
175 g/6 oz/¾ cup caster (superfine) sugar

15 ml/1 tbsp cornflour (cornstarch)
150 ml/¼ pt/⅔ cup crème de cassis
150 ml/¼ pt/⅔ cup single (light) cream
Ground cinnamon, for dusting

1   Strip the currants from their stalks and place in a saucepan. Add the water and lemon rind and bring to the boil.

2   Lower the heat, cover and simmer gently for 20 minutes.

3   Add the sugar and stir until dissolved. Leave to cool to lukewarm.

4   Blend in two or three batches until smooth, then transfer to a clean saucepan.

5   Mix the cornflour to a smooth paste with the crème de cassis. Stir into the pan, then bring gently to the boil and simmer for 1 minute until the soup is slightly thickened.

6   Pour into a bowl and place a round of damp greaseproof (waxed) paper directly on top of the soup. Leave to cool, then chill for several hours until very cold.

7   Before serving, remove the greaseproof paper (any layer of skin will come away with it), stir round and pour into six bowls. Drizzle the cream over each portion and dust with cinnamon.

PREPARATION TIME: 15 MINUTES
COOKING TIME: 25 MINUTES

This Scandinavian-inspired soup is slightly sharp and has a beautiful crimson colour. It is ideal to serve as a starter, especially if you are serving poultry or game after as a main dish, making it perfect for Christmas dinner.

scandinavian cranberry wine soup

SERVES 6

450 g/1 lb fresh or frozen
  cranberries
750 ml/1¼ pts/3 cups water
15 ml/1 tbsp grated orange rind
275 g/10 oz/1¼ cups caster
  (superfine) sugar

15 ml/1 tbsp cornflour (cornstarch)
150 ml/¼ pt/⅔ cup red wine
150 ml/¼ pt/⅔ cup single (light)
  cream
Ground allspice, for dusting

1 Place the cranberries in a saucepan with the water and orange rind. Bring to the boil.

2 Lower the heat, cover and simmer gently for 20 minutes.

3 Remove from the heat, add the sugar and stir until dissolved. Leave to cool to lukewarm.

4 Blend in two or three batches until smooth, then transfer to a clean saucepan.

5 Mix the cornflour to a smooth paste with the wine. Stir into the pan, then bring gently to the boil and simmer for 1 minute until the soup is slightly thickened.

6 Pour into a bowl and place a round of damp greaseproof (waxed) paper directly on top of the soup. Leave to cool, then chill for several hours until very cold.

7 Before serving, remove the greaseproof paper (any layer of skin will come away with it), stir round and pour into six bowls. Drizzle the cream over each portion and dust with allspice.

PREPARATION TIME: 15 MINUTES
COOKING TIME: 25 MINUTES

The ever-popular fruit combination of apples and blackberries is brought together in this recipe to create a zesty autumnal soup. Serve with a slice of warmed crusty bread smothered in melted butter for a delicious main meal.

autumn apple and blackberry soup

SERVES 6

350 g/12 oz cooking (tart) apples, peeled, cored and sliced
225 g/8 oz blackberries
750 ml/1¼ pts/3 cups water
10 ml/2 tsp grated lemon rind
225 g/8 oz/1 cup caster (superfine) sugar

15 ml/1 tbsp cornflour (cornstarch)
150 ml/¼ pt/⅔ cup sweet cider
150 ml/¼ pt/⅔ cup single (light) cream
Ground cinnamon, for dusting

1 Place the apples and blackberries in a saucepan with the water and lemon rind. Bring to the boil.

2 Lower the heat, cover and simmer gently for 20 minutes.

3 Remove from the heat, add the sugar and stir until dissolved. Leave to cool to lukewarm.

4 Blend in two or three batches until smooth, then transfer to a clean saucepan.

5 Mix the cornflour to a smooth paste with the cider. Stir into the pan, then bring gently to the boil and simmer for 1 minute until the soup is slightly thickened.

6 Pour into a bowl and place a round of damp greaseproof (waxed) paper directly on top of the soup, Leave to cool, then chill for several hours until very cold.

7 Before serving, remove the greaseproof paper (any layer of skin will come away with it), stir round and pour into six bowls. Drizzle the cream over each portion and dust with cinnamon.

PREPARATION TIME: 15 MINUTES
COOKING TIME: 25 MINUTES

This is an excellent way of making sure you get your five-a-day. Ogen melon is a very sweet fruit that was originally developed in Israel. If you are unable to purchase an Ogen, substitute it with any sweet-flavoured melon, such as Honeydew.

mixed fruit soup with a wee dram

SERVES 4

600 ml/1 pt/2½ cups fresh orange juice
60 ml/4 tbsp caster (superfine) sugar
45 ml/3 tbsp sultanas (golden raisins)
½ ogen melon

1 large orange
1 ripe pear, peeled, cored and chopped
1 eating (dessert) apple, peeled, cored and chopped
15 ml/1 tbsp cornflour (cornstarch)
30 ml/2 tbsp whisky or water

1 Place the orange juice, sugar and sultanas in a saucepan. Leave to stand while preparing the fruit.

2 Remove the seeds from the melon, then scoop the flesh and juice directly into the saucepan.

3 Peel the orange and cut the flesh into chunks, removing the pips. Add the orange flesh to the pan with the pear and apple.

4 Bring to the boil, then lower the heat. Cover and simmer gently for 40 minutes.

5 Leave to cool to lukewarm, then blend in two batches until smooth. Transfer to a clean saucepan.

6 Mix the cornflour to a smooth paste with the whisky or water, add to the soup and bring back to the boil. Lower the heat and cook for 1 minute.

7 Place a round of damp greaseproof (waxed) paper directly on top of the soup. Leave to cool, then chill for several hours until very cold.

8 Before serving, remove the greaseproof paper (any layer of skin will come away with it), stir and pour into bowls to serve.

PREPARATION TIME: 30 MINUTES
COOKING TIME: 45–50 MINUTES

To get the best flavour from this unusual soup, use a good-quality cider – there are many brands available in the supermarkets nowadays. This is best served with ginger snaps or almond biscuits (cookies).

spiced apricot and cider soup with honey

SERVES 6

250 g/9 oz/1½ cups dried apricots
600 ml/1 pt/2½ cups water
300 ml/½ pt/1¼ cups medium-sweet
   cider

60 ml/4 tbsp clear honey
45 ml/3 tbsp lemon juice
Juice of 1 lime
1.5 ml/¼ tsp ground allspice

1   Soak the apricots in water as directed on the packet.

2   Drain and transfer to a saucepan with half the water and all the remaining ingredients. Bring gently to the boil.

3   Lower the heat, cover and simmer gently for 40 minutes.

4   Leave to cool to lukewarm, then blend in two batches until smooth.

5   Transfer to a large bowl and stir in the remaining water until smooth.

6   Cover and chill for several hours until very cold.

7   Stir before serving.

PREPARATION TIME: 10 MINUTES, PLUS SOAKING TIME
COOKING TIME: 45 MINUTES

Another healthy option full of fibre and vitamins A and C. It is believed Cleopatra used rosewater to keep her looking beautiful so the addition of this exquisitely scented water means this soup will keep you looking and feeling great!

apricot and apple
rose-scented soup

SERVES 4

100 g/4 oz/²/₃ cup dried apricots
175 g/6 oz cooking (tart) apples, peeled, cored and sliced
300 ml/¹/₂ pt/1¼ cups freshly pressed apple juice

75 ml/5 tbsp water
15 ml/1 tbsp rose water
15 ml/1 tbsp apricot brandy

1 Soak the apricots in water as directed on the packet.

2 Drain and transfer to a saucepan with the apple slices, apple juice and water. Bring to the boil.

3 Lower the heat, cover and simmer gently for 15 minutes.

4 Leave to cool to lukewarm, then blend in two or three batches until smooth.

5 Transfer to a bowl and stir in the rose water and apricot brandy. Cover and chill thoroughly.

6 Stir before serving.

PREPARATION TIME: 15 MINUTES, PLUS SOAKING TIME

CANNED
FRUIT
SOUPS

Canned fruit fillings – more often used in flans, pies and tarts and on cheesecakes – are an effortless way of making luscious soups at reasonable cost. Most are vividly coloured and can transform a simple meal into a banquet. The origins of fruit soups lie in Central and Northern Europe, where they are served ice-cold as a starter or snack throughout the summer months, often with a topping of milk or cream.

rhubarb, redcurrant and grape juice soup

100 g/4 oz redcurrants
600 ml/1 pt/2½ cups red grape juice
400 g/14 oz/1 large can of rhubarb
    fruit filling

150 ml/¼ pt/⅔ cup water
60 ml/4 tbsp single (light) cream

1 Strip the redcurrants from their stalks and place in the blender with half the grape juice. Blend until smooth.

2 Add the fruit filling and blend for 12 seconds.

3 Transfer to a bowl, stir in the remaining grape juice and the water, then cover and chill.

4 Stir before serving with a little cream drizzled over each portion.

PREPARATION TIME: 10 MINUTES

apple and sparkling perry soup

SERVES 4

400 g/14 oz/1 large can of apple
    fruit filling
450 ml/¾ pt/2 cups sparkling perry
    (pear cider)

15 ml/1 tbsp apricot jam (conserve)
2.5 ml/½ tsp ground cinnamon

1 Blend the fruit filling with half the perry, the apricot jam and cinnamon for about 12 seconds until fairly smooth.

2 Transfer to a bowl and stir in the remaining perry. Cover and chill.

3 Stir before serving.

PREPARATION TIME: 5 MINUTES

red cherry and raspberry soup with cranberry and rose water

SERVES 4–5

400 g/14 oz/1 large can of red
  cherry fruit filling
100 g/4 oz raspberries

600 ml/1 pt/2½ cups cranberry juice
15 ml/1 tbsp rose water

1 Blend the fruit filling with the raspberries for about 12 seconds until fairly smooth.

2 Transfer to a bowl and stir in the cranberry juice and rose water. Cover and chill.

3 Stir before serving.

PREPARATION TIME: 5 MINUTES

apricot and mandarin orange soup with amaretto di saronno

SERVES 4–5

350 g/12 oz/1 medium can of
  mandarin oranges in light syrup
400 g/14 oz/1 large can of apricot
  fruit filling

300 ml/1/2 pt/1¼ cups water
30 ml/2 tbsp amaretto di saronno

1 Blend the contents of the can of mandarin oranges with all the remaining ingredients for about 15 seconds until fairly smooth.

2 Cover and chill.

3 Stir before serving.

PREPARATION TIME: 5 MINUTES

black cherry and red wine soup

SERVES 4–5

400 g/14 oz/1 large can of black
   cherry fruit filling
30 ml/2 tbsp sour cherry fruit syrup

300 ml/½ pt/1¼ cups red wine
150 ml/¼ pt/⅔ cup water
5 ml/1 tsp angostura bitters

1 Blend the fruit filling, fruit syrup and half the wine for about 15 seconds until fairly smooth. Pour into a bowl.

2 Stir in the remaining wine, the water and angostura bitters.

3 Cover and chill.

4 Stir before serving.

PREPARATION TIME: 5 MINUTES

blackcurrant and apple juice soup

SERVES 4–5

400 g/14 oz/1 large can of
   blackcurrant fruit filling

600 ml/1 pt/2½ cups apple juice
60 ml/4 tbsp double (heavy) cream

1 Blend the fruit filling with half the apple juice for about 10 seconds until fairly smooth.

2 Transfer to a bowl and stir in the remaining apple juice. Cover and chill.

3 Stir before serving with a little cream drizzled over each portion.

PREPARATION TIME: 10 MINUTES

VEGETABLE
SOUPS

This chapter offers the biggest selection
of all, featuring every conceivable kind
of vegetable – including salad greens – to
give you infinite variety and plenty of choice
whether you are looking for casual eating or
more formal dining.

This is simply a variation of cauliflower cheese that works well as a soup. It makes quite a hearty dish on its own but for larger appetites, serve the soup with brown bread and butter or savoury crackers for a satisfying meal.

cauliflower, cheese and buttermilk soup

SERVES 4–6

225 g/8 oz cauliflower florets
600 ml/1 pt/2½ cups vegetable
  stock
A pinch of salt
15 ml/1 tbsp cornflour (cornstarch)
30 ml/2 tbsp water
300 ml/½ pt/1¼ cups cultured
  buttermilk

5–10 ml/1–2 tsp made mustard
10 ml/2 tsp lemon juice
100 g/4 oz/1 cup Cheddar cheese,
  grated
Salt and freshly ground black pepper
30 ml/2 tbsp chopped parsley

1 Place the cauliflower florets in a large pan with the stock and salt. Bring to the boil, then lower the heat and cover the pan. Simmer for about 20 minutes until the cauliflower is soft.

2 Remove from the heat and leave to cool to lukewarm.

3 Blend in two batches until smooth, then transfer to a clean saucepan.

4 Mix the cornflour to a smooth paste with the water, then stir into the pan with the buttermilk, mustard and lemon juice.

5 Bring to the boil over a medium–low heat, stirring continuously, then simmer gently for 2 minutes until thickened.

6 Add the cheese and stir gently until melted. Season to taste with salt and pepper.

7 Serve very hot, sprinkled with the parsley.

PREPARATION TIME: 10 MINUTES
COOKING TIME: 30 MINUTES

Broccoli is a highly nutritious vegetable and combined with almonds serves to give you a real boost of vitamins A, C and E, as well as fibre. Combined with Stilton, this soup is healthy yet rich and creamy. Add croûtons for texture.

broccoli and stilton soup with toasted almonds

SERVES 4–5

25 g/1 oz/¼ cup flaked (slivered) almonds
450 g/1 lb broccoli, cut into pieces
750 ml/1¼ pts/3 cups water
5 ml/1 tsp salt

450 ml/¾ pt/2 cups skimmed milk
5 ml/1 tsp cornflour (cornstarch)
10 ml/2 tsp water
50 g/2 oz/½ cup Stilton cheese, crumbled

1 Toast the almond flakes in a dry frying pan (skillet) over a low heat, turning often. Transfer to a plate and leave to cool.

2 Place the broccoli in a pan with the larger quantity of water and the salt. Bring to the boil.

3 Lower the heat, cover and simmer for 20–25 minutes or until soft. Leave to cool to lukewarm.

4 Blend in two batches until smooth, then transfer to a clean saucepan. Add the milk.

5 Mix the cornflour smoothly with the smaller quantity of water, then stir into the pan.

6 Bring just to the boil, stirring, then simmer gently for 2 minutes.

7 Add the cheese and stir until melted.

8 Serve hot, sprinkling each portion with the toasted almonds.

PREPARATION TIME: 15 MINUTES
COOKING TIME: 30 MINUTES

This is a distinctive and vibrant soup, akin to ratatouille, seasoned with balsamic vinegar. For a satisfying main meal, serve the soup with chunks of granary bread or a baguette with a side dish of thinly sliced salami.

mediterranean summer vegetable soup

SERVES 6–8

15 ml/1 tbsp olive oil
2 onions, thinly sliced
3 garlic cloves, thinly sliced
2 green (bell) peppers, halved and seeded
450 g/1 lb courgettes (zucchini), sliced

450 g/1 lb tomatoes, blanched, skinned and quartered
350 g/12 oz aubergine (eggplant), diced
1.5 litres/2½ pts/6 cups water
A pinch of salt
45 ml/3 tbsp balsamic vinegar
Freshly ground black pepper
30–40 ml/6–8 tsp pesto

1 Heat the oil in a large saucepan. Add the onions and garlic and fry (sauté) until golden brown.

2 Add the vegetables, water and salt and bring to the boil.

3 Lower the heat, cover and cook gently for 35–40 minutes or until soft. Leave to cool to lukewarm.

4 Blend in three batches until just blended or smooth, as you prefer, then transfer to a clean saucepan.

5 Reheat until hot, stir in the vinegar and season with black pepper.

6 Serve in individual bowls, adding 5 ml/1 tsp of pesto to each portion immediately before serving.

PREPARATION TIME: 30 MINUTES
COOKING TIME: 45 MINUTES

This is an elegant variation on a firm traditional favourite. Tomato soup lends itself to experimentation so try serving this soup over rice for a hearty Eastern European meal or use grated Parmesan instead of the Mozzarella.

italian tomato and mozzarella soup

SERVES 6

100 g/4 oz/1 cup Mozzarella cheese, cubed
900 ml/1½ pts/3¾ cups tomato juice
15 ml/1 tbsp pesto
30 ml/2 tbsp sun-dried tomato purée (paste)
15 ml/1 tbsp cornflour (cornstarch)
5 ml/1 tsp chopped fresh basil leaves
75 ml/5 tbsp rosé wine
150 ml/¼ pt/⅔ cup water
10–15 ml/2–3 tsp caster (superfine) sugar
A few fresh basil leaves, for garnishing

1 Place the cheese in the blender with half the tomato juice, the pesto, tomato purée, cornflour and chopped basil. Blend until very smooth. Transfer to a large saucepan.

2 Mix in the remaining tomato juice with the wine, water and sugar to taste.

3 Cook gently, stirring, over a low heat until the soup comes to the boil and thickens.

4 Simmer for 2 minutes, then serve piping hot garnished with basil leaves.

PREPARATION TIME: 10 MINUTES
COOKING TIME: 10–15 MINUTES

A taste of the Mediterranean, this warming soup encompasses the mild but delicious flavour of fried aubergine with aromatic toasted pine nuts. For the best results, try buying the aubergine in July as this is when it is naturally in season.

aromatic aubergine soup with pine nuts

SERVES 8

40 ml/8 tsp pine nuts
30 ml/2 tbsp groundnut (peanut) oil
700 g/1½ lb aubergine (eggplant), unpeeled and cubed
225 g/8 oz onions, chopped

1.5 litres/2½ pts/6 cups water
Juice of 1 large lemon
30 ml/2 tbsp tomato purée (paste)
Salt and freshly ground black pepper

1 Toast the pine nuts in a dry frying pan until lightly golden. Set aside.

2 Heat the oil in a large saucepan until sizzling, then add the aubergines and onions.

3 Fry (sauté) gently for 40 minutes, tossing occasionally and keeping the pan covered for the first 20 minutes, then uncovering to evaporate the moisture.

4 Add half the water, the lemon juice and tomato purée and season with salt and pepper. Bring to the boil.

5 Lower the heat, cover and simmer gently for 30 minutes. Leave to cool to lukewarm.

6 Blend in one or two batches until smooth, then transfer to a clean saucepan.

7 Add the remaining water and reheat.

8 Serve hot, sprinkling 5 ml/1 tsp of the pine nuts on each serving.

PREPARATION TIME: 30 MINUTES

COOKING TIME: 1¼ HOURS

An unusual twist on an old favourite with whipped egg whites creating a delicious foamy texture. To complete the cappuccino experience, serve this soup in cups and saucers with a teaspoon in the saucer for scooping up all the froth.

mushroom cappuccino with nutmeg

SERVES 6–8

350 g/12 oz mushrooms
30 ml/2 tbsp melted butter
30 ml/2 tbsp plain (all-purpose) flour
750 ml/1¼ pts/3 cups skimmed milk

5 ml/1 tsp salt, plus a pinch for whipping
1.5 ml/¼ tsp grated nutmeg
2 eggs, separated

1 Break up the mushrooms directly into the blender.

2 Add the butter, flour and half the milk. Blend to a semi-smooth purée, then transfer to a saucepan.

3 Add the remaining milk, the salt and nutmeg. Heat gently, stirring, until the soup comes to the boil and thickens.

4 Beat the egg yolks into the hot soup, then remove from the heat.

5 Whip the egg whites to a stiff snow with a pinch of salt, then whisk evenly into the soup.

6 Pour into cups and serve straight away.

PREPARATION TIME: 15 MINUTES
COOKING TIME: 10 MINUTES

Ginger root is widely known for having excellent medicinal benefits. When used in cooking it gives a warming, biting flavour which, in this soup, is offset by milder ingredients such as crème fraîche. Excellent for when you need an energy boost.

mushroom soup
with fresh ginger

SERVES 6–7

150 g/5 oz onions, finely chopped
25 g/1 oz fresh root ginger, finely
  chopped
25 g/1 oz/2 tbsp butter
7.5 ml/1½ tsp olive oil

1 kg/2¼ lb mushrooms, sliced
1 litre/1¾ pts/4¼ cups hot vegetable
  stock
150 ml/¼ pt/⅔ cup crème fraîche
30 ml/2 tbsp tomato purée (paste)

1   Fry (sauté) the onions and ginger gently in the butter and oil in a large saucepan for 7 minutes until pale golden brown.

2   Add the mushrooms to the pan and fry for a further 7 minutes, turning frequently.

3   Add the stock and bring to the boil.

4   Lower the heat, cover and simmer for 7 minutes. Leave to cool to lukewarm.

5   Add the crème fraîche and tomato purée and reheat gently without boiling, stirring from time to time.

6   Serve hot.

PREPARATION TIME: 15 MINUTES
COOKING TIME: 25 MINUTES

This is a version of Shchi, a warming and hearty soup that is
traditional in Russia and popular in Eastern Europe. It makes a
filling meal on its own when served with dark rye bread.
Blending only half the soup gives it an interesting texture.

russian-style cabbage and tomato soup

SERVES 6–8

450 g/1 lb white cabbage, finely
   shredded
1 large onion, chopped
225 g/8 oz tomatoes, blanched,
   skinned and chopped

1 litre/1¾ pts/4¼ cups vegetable
   stock
5 ml/1 tsp dried herbs
Salt and freshly ground black pepper
150 ml/¼ pt/⅔ cup soured (dairy
   sour) cream

1 Place all the ingredients except the seasoning and soured cream in a saucepan.

2 Bring to the boil, stirring from time to time, then cover and simmer gently for 45 minutes. Leave to cool to lukewarm.

3 Transfer only half the soup to a blender and blend until smooth.

4 Return to the pan and reheat until very hot, stirring periodically. Season to taste with salt and pepper.

5 Serve hot, topping each portion with plenty of soured cream.

PREPARATION TIME: 20 MINUTES
COOKING TIME: 50 MINUTES

A French speciality that is closely related to minestrone. A condiment called pistou (the locals' name for basil) is stirred into the soup at the last moment to provide a delicious aromatic touch. Pistou is similar to pesto but does not contain pine nuts.

provençal vegetable pistou soup

SERVES 6–8

FOR THE PISTOU:
12 fresh basil leaves
175 g/6 oz Parmesan cheese,
   roughly chopped
4 garlic cloves
60–90 ml/4–6 tbsp olive oil

FOR THE SOUP:
100 g/4 oz/⅔ cup dried haricot
   (navy) beans, soaked overnight
2 leeks, halved lengthways

1 onion, coarsely chopped
1 courgette (zucchini), unpeeled and
   sliced
2 potatoes, peeled and diced
3 tomatoes, coarsely chopped
2 celery stalks, sliced
225 g/8 oz frozen sliced French
   (green) beans
1.2 litres/2 pts/5 cups water
50 g/2 oz cooked macaroni

1 To make the pistou, place the basil, Parmesan and garlic in a small blender and, with the machine running, gradually trickle in the olive oil through the hole in the top of the lid to form a creamy leaf-green paste. Set aside.

2 To make the soup, drain the haricot beans and place in a saucepan with plenty of cold water.

3 Bring to the boil and keep boiling fairly briskly for 10 minutes, then part-cover and simmer for 40 minutes. Drain and set aside.

4 Place all the vegetables in a large saucepan with half the haricot beans and the measured water. Bring to the boil, then cover and simmer for 1 hour or until the beans are soft. Leave to cool to lukewarm.

5 Blend in two or three batches to a coarse and chunky purée, then transfer to a clean saucepan. Add the remaining haricot beans and the macaroni and reheat until very hot.

6 Stir in 45 ml/3 tbsp of the pistou and serve straight away.

note:

Any leftover pistou can be kept in a screw-topped jar in the refrigerator for up to 3 weeks.

PREPARATION TIME: 15–20 MINUTES FOR THE PISTOU;

30 MINUTES FOR THE SOUP

COOKING TIME: 2–2½ HOURS

Another French-influenced recipe that makes the most of sweet young turnips that are at their best during the winter months, in particular January. Try varying the taste by experimenting with different types of potato, such as sweet potatoes.

cream of sweet turnip soup

SERVES 4–5

For the croûtons:
4 large slices of white bread, crusts removed
30–45 ml/2–3 tbsp melted butter or oil

FOR THE SOUP:
225 g/8 oz turnips, peeled and chopped

225 g/8 oz potatoes, peeled and chopped
175 g/6 oz onions, chopped
1 litre/1¾ pts/4¼ cups water
Salt and freshly ground black pepper
150 ml/¼ pt/⅔ cup single (light) cream

1 To make the croûtons, cut the bread into small cubes and toss in a bowl with the butter or oil.

2 Transfer to a large frying pan and fry over a medium heat, turning occasionally, until golden brown and crispy. Transfer to a plate and leave to cool.

3 To make the soup, place the turnips, potatoes and onions in a saucepan with the water and salt.

4 Bring to the boil, then cover and simmer for about 40 minutes or until the vegetables are soft. Leave to cool to lukewarm.

5 Blend in two or three batches until very smooth, then transfer to a clean saucepan.

6 Add the cream and reheat, stirring, until hot. Season to taste with salt and pepper.

7 Serve with a sprinkling of the croûtons in each portion.

PREPARATION TIME: 15 MINUTES
COOKING TIME: 1 HOUR

An absolute classic that all too often seems to be forgotten about as people pick from the array of canned varieties that supermarkets offer. Nothing beats making tomato soup from scratch, especially using flavoursome tomatoes in season.

traditional
fresh tomato soup

SERVES 6

75 g/3 oz lean bacon rashers
(slices), chopped
75 g/3 oz carrots, chopped
175 g/6 oz red onions, chopped
1 celery stalk, chopped
20 ml/1½ tbsp sunflower oil
900 g/2 lb ripe tomatoes, blanched,
skinned and coarsely chopped

900 ml/1½ pts/3¾ cups vegetable
stock
30 ml/2 tbsp tomato purée (paste)
15 ml/1 tbsp brown sugar
5 ml/1 tsp salt
1 bay leaf
15 ml/1 tbsp cornflour (cornstarch)
60 ml/4 tbsp cold water
A little single (light) cream

1 Gently fry the bacon, carrots, onions and celery in the oil in a large saucepan until lightly browned.

2 Add the tomatoes, stock, tomato purée, sugar, salt and bay leaf. Bring to the boil, stirring.

3 Lower the heat, cover and simmer for 1 hour. Leave to cool to lukewarm.

4 Remove the bay leaf. If you want a smooth soup, blend in two or three batches until smooth. Transfer to a clean saucepan.

5 Mix the cornflour to a smooth paste with the water and add to the pan.

6 Bring to the boil and simmer gently for 2 minutes.

7 Serve hot, with a little cream trickled over each portion.

PREPARATION TIME: 30 MINUTES
COOKING TIME: 1¼ HOURS

An economical soup that makes the most of the winter vegetables on offer. Eat this to warm and nourish yourself on cold, bleak days. Serve with thick buttered slices of granary bread for a healthy and filling lunchtime meal.

creamy potato, carrot and leek soup

SERVES 6

450 g/1 lb potatoes, peeled and
    diced
225 g/8 oz carrots, diced
3 large leeks, halved lengthways and
    diced

1 litre/1¾ pts/4¼ cups water
5 ml/1 tsp salt
450 ml/¾ pt/2 cups full cream milk
Shredded fresh flatleaf parsley, to
    garnish

1 Place the potatoes, carrots and leeks in a saucepan with the water and salt. Bring to the boil.

2 Lower the heat, cover and simmer for 40 minutes or until the vegetables are tender. Leave to cool to lukewarm.

3 Stir in the milk, then reheat until hot.

4 Garnish each serving with shreds of parsley.

PREPARATION TIME: 20 MINUTES
COOKING TIME: 40 MINUTES

Lentils are available throughout the year and are cheap and easy to prepare. Lentils have enormous nutritional value, being low in calories but high in fibre, vitamins and minerals. They easily absorb other flavours and provide a tasty meal.

curried lentil soup with carrots and onions

SERVES 6–8

15 ml/1 tbsp sunflower oil
100 g/4 oz onions, thinly sliced
100 g/4 oz carrots, thinly sliced
15 ml/1 tbsp medium-hot curry
   powder
175 g/6 oz/1 cup red lentils

2.5 ml/½ tsp paprika
1.2 litres/2 pts/5 cups hot water
2 large slices of brown bread,
   crumbed
Ground cumin, for dusting

1 Heat the oil in a saucepan until sizzling. Add the onions and carrots and fry for 10 minutes or until lightly golden.

2 Stir in the curry powder and cook for 1 minute, stirring all the time.

3 Stir in the lentils, paprika and water. Bring to the boil, stirring.

4 Lower the heat, cover and simmer for 40 minutes, stirring from time to time and adding a little more hot water if the soup seems to be thickening too much. Leave to cool to lukewarm.

5 Blend in two batches until smooth, then transfer to a clean saucepan.

6 Stir in the breadcrumbs, then reheat until boiling.

7 Serve straight away with a dusting of cumin on each portion.

PREPARATION TIME: 15 MINUTES
COOKING TIME: 1 HOUR

Although this combination is usually used for jam, it is equally delicious served as a creamy soup. Marrow has a wonderful texture but is quite mild flavoured so benefits from being mixed with the sparky piquancy of ginger.

creamy marrow and ginger soup

SERVES 6

FOR THE GARLIC CROÛTONS:
4 large slices of white bread, crusts removed
30–45 ml/2–3 tbsp melted butter or oil
2 garlic cloves, crushed

FOR THE SOUP:
1.5 kg/3 lb marrow

100 g/4 oz onions, sliced
900 ml/1½ pts/3¾ cups water
15 g/½ oz fresh root ginger, peeled and thinly sliced
5 ml/1 tsp salt
250 g/9 oz German quark or crème fraîche

1 To make the croûtons, cut the bread into small cubes and toss in a bowl with the butter or oil and the garlic.

2 Transfer to a large frying pan and fry over a medium heat, turning occasionally, until golden brown and crispy. Transfer to a plate and leave to cool.

3 To make the soup, peel and slice the marrow, removing the seeds and fibres. Cut the marrow slices into chunks. Place in a saucepan with the onions, water, ginger and salt.

4 Bring gently to the boil, then lower the heat, cover and simmer gently for 30 minutes or until the vegetables are soft. Leave to cool to lukewarm.

5 Stir in the quark or crème fraîche, then blend in two or three batches until smooth. Transfer to a clean saucepan and reheat gently without boiling.

6 Serve with a topping of the garlic croûtons on each portion.

PREPARATION TIME: 25 MINUTES
COOKING TIME: 40 MINUTES

A colourful and sweet soup, healthily thickened with fibrous brown rice flakes. If you are unable to source yellow courgettes or rice flakes, simply use ordinary green courgettes and substitute with brown basmati rice instead.

yellow courgette soup with onions and rice flakes

SERVES 6

550 g/1¼ lb yellow courgettes (zucchini), thinly sliced
175 g/6 oz onions, coarsely chopped
15 ml/1 tbsp groundnut (peanut) oil
1 litre/1¾ pts/4¼ cups water
5–10 ml/1–2 tsp salt
90 ml/6 tbsp brown rice flakes
150 ml/¼ pt/⅔ cup full cream milk
1.5 ml/¼ tsp grated nutmeg

1 Fry the courgettes and onions in the oil in a saucepan for about 8 minutes until lightly golden.

2 Add the water, salt and rice flakes. Bring gently to the boil, stirring.

3 Lower the heat, cover and simmer for 30 minutes. Leave to cool to lukewarm.

4 Blend in two or three batches to a coarse purée, then transfer to a clean saucepan.

5 Stir in the milk and nutmeg and reheat until hot before serving.

PREPARATION TIME: 15 MINUTES
COOKING TIME: 45 MINUTES

Butternut squash has a wonderfully succulent and sweet flesh that is ideal for using in soups. The vibrant golden colour ensures that it makes an attractive starter. Serve with freshly baked rosemary focaccia.

butternut squash and peanut butter soup

SERVES 6

45 ml/3 tbsp flaked (slivered) almonds
700 g/1½ lb butternut squash
600 ml/1 pt/2½ cups vegetable stock

60 ml/4 tbsp crunchy peanut butter
250 ml/8 fl oz/1 cup buttermilk
1.5 ml/¼ tsp grated nutmeg
2.5 ml/½ tsp salt

1 Toast the almond flakes in a dry frying pan (skillet) over a low heat, turning often. Transfer to a plate and leave to cool.

2 Halve the squash, leaving in the seeds, and place on a microwave plate, cut-sides down. Cook on full power for 15 minutes or until you can easily pierce through the skin and into the flesh with a wooden cocktail stick (toothpick).

3 Leave to cool to lukewarm, then scoop out the seeds and fibres with a spoon and discard. Remove the flesh as close to the skin as possible and place in the blender.

4 Blend with all the remaining ingredients except the almonds until smooth. Transfer to a saucepan and heat until hot but not boiling.

5 Sprinkle each portion with the almonds and serve.

PREPARATION TIME: 10 MINUTES
COOKING TIME: 20 MINUTES

Evoking the essence of autumn, this soup has a mild and delicate flavour that looks more lavish and expensive than it actually is! If you have difficulty locating chestnuts, try local health food shops or organic stores instead of supermarkets.

milky chestnut and onion soup

SERVES 6

450 g/1 lb frozen chestnuts, defrosted
100 g/4 oz onions, sliced

900 ml/1½ pts/3¾ cups skimmed milk
5 ml/1 tsp salt
Ground allspice, for sprinkling

1 Place the chestnuts and onions in a saucepan with the milk and salt. Bring gently to the boil.

2 Lower the heat, part-cover and simmer gently for 30 minutes. Leave to cool to lukewarm.

3 Blend in two batches until smooth, then transfer to a clean saucepan.

4 Reheat until hot, then serve with a dusting of allspice on each portion.

PREPARATION TIME: 10 MINUTES
COOKING TIME: 40 MINUTES

An ideal soup for those watching their weight as it is light and tasty with just the smallest amount of butter added at the end to boost the flavour. For best results, make and eat the soup on the same day.

cucumber, green pepper and celery soup

SERVES 4–5

225 g/8 oz cucumber, peeled and thinly sliced
100 g/4 oz green (bell) pepper, seeded and cut into strips
3 large celery stalks, chopped
300 ml/½ pt/1¼ cups water
15 ml/1 tbsp cider vinegar
15 ml/1 tbsp cornflour (cornstarch)
2.5 ml/½ tsp mustard powder
2.5 ml/½ tsp salt
300 ml/½ pt/1¼ cups skimmed milk
10 ml/2 tsp butter
30 ml/2 tbsp finely chopped fresh parsley

1   Place the cucumber, pepper and celery in a blender with the water, vinegar, cornflour, mustard powder and salt. Blend until very smooth.

2   Transfer to a saucepan and stir in the milk.

3   Cook, stirring, until the soup comes to the boil and thickens, then simmer for 5 minutes. Stir in the butter.

4   Serve with a sprinkling of parsley on each portion.

PREPARATION TIME: 20 MINUTES
COOKING TIME: 10 MINUTES

Peas are a great superfood, providing lots of fibre, vitamins and minerals. Their wonderful green colour means that this soup is both striking and very nutritious. Try adding some freshly chopped mint just before blending, for a delicious change.

quick and easy
green pea soup

SERVES 6

450 g/1 lb frozen peas
1 litre/1¾ pts/4¼ cups vegetable
  stock
5 ml/1 tsp salt

10 ml/2 tsp cornflour (cornstarch)
15 ml/1 tbsp water
60 ml/4 tbsp single (light) cream

1 Place the peas in a large saucepan with the stock and salt.

2 Mix the cornflour to a smooth paste with the water and pour into the pan. Bring to the boil.

3 Lower the heat and simmer, uncovered, for 3–4 minutes. Leave to cool to lukewarm.

4 Blend in two or three batches until smooth, then transfer to a clean saucepan.

5 Reheat before serving with a swirl of cream in each portion.

PREPARATION TIME: 5 MINUTES
COOKING TIME: 7 MINUTES

This soup is excellent for an outdoor supper in the summer, especially as it is so quick and easy to make. Save some cream to swirl on the soup after you have ladled it into bowls ready to serve for attractive presentation.

green pea and lettuce soup with coriander

SERVES 8

4 little gem lettuces, shredded
450 g/1 lb frozen peas
25 g/1 oz fresh coriander (cilantro)
   leaves
30 ml/2 tbsp melted butter

5 ml/1 tsp olive oil
1.4 litres/2¼ pts/scant 6 cups water
Salt and freshly ground black pepper
150 ml/¼ pt/⅔ cup single (light)
   cream

1   Place the lettuces, peas and coriander in a large saucepan.

2   Add the butter and oil and toss gently until coated, then add the water.

3   Bring to the boil, then lower the heat, cover and simmer for 20 minutes. Leave to cool to lukewarm.

4   Blend in two or three batches until smooth, then transfer to a clean saucepan and season with salt and pepper. Reheat until very hot.

5   Immediately before serving, remove the pan from the heat and stir in the cream.

PREPARATION TIME: 10 MINUTES
COOKING TIME: 25 MINUTES

Artichoke hearts are delicious but can be difficult to cut from the artichoke. Using canned hearts means that there is much less work to do but the result is still a very elegant, delicate soup with a slightly sharp taste.

smooth artichoke soup hollandaise

SERVES 4–5

400 g/14 oz/1 large can of artichoke hearts
450 ml/¾ pt/2 cups semi-skimmed milk
10 ml/2 tsp plain (all-purpose) flour
2.5 ml/½ tsp salt
15 g/½ oz/1 tbsp butter
2 egg yolks
15 ml/1 tbsp fresh lemon juice

1 Place the contents of the can of artichokes in the blender. Add the milk, flour and salt and blend until smooth. Transfer to a saucepan.

2 Cook over a low heat, stirring all the time, until the soup comes to the boil and thickens slightly.

3 Add the butter. Simmer for 3 minutes on the lowest possible heat, then remove the pan from the heat and allow the soup to cool slightly.

4 Place a ladleful of soup in a small bowl and mix in the egg yolks and lemon juice (this prevents curdling).

5 Tip this mixture back into the pan of soup and stir in gently. Serve straight away.

PREPARATION TIME: 10 MINUTES

COOKING TIME: 10 MINUTES

Inspired by the Mediterranean, this soup is dark, a little smoky in flavour and coarsely textured. The faint taste of sweet-sour derives from the balsamic vinegar. This is a marvellous soup to precede a French or Italian dish.

lentil soup with red onions and porcini mushrooms

SERVES 4–5

350 g/12 oz red onions, coarsely chopped
25 g/1 oz sun-dried (bell) peppers, rinsed and cut into strips
2 garlic cloves, coarsely chopped
175 g/6 oz/1 cup puy lentils, rinsed
1.5 litre/2½ pts/6 cups water
15 g/½ oz dried porcini mushrooms
50 g/2 oz soft sun-dried tomatoes
60 ml/4 tbsp balsamic vinegar
Freshly grated Parmesan cheese, for sprinkling

1 Place the onions, peppers and garlic in a large saucepan with the lentils and water.

2 Break pieces of the mushrooms directly into the pan (it is not necessary to soak them first). Bring to the boil.

3 Reduce the heat until the water bubbles noticeably but not vigorously. Continue to cook, uncovered, for 25–30 minutes or until the lentils look fairly swollen and the soup is thick.

4 Blend only half the soup until smooth, then return to the saucepan. Break in the sun-dried tomatoes and add the balsamic vinegar.

5 Reheat and serve very hot with a bowl of Parmesan handed separately.

PREPARATION TIME: 15 MINUTES
COOKING TIME: 35 MINUTES

Another quick recipe that provides a full-flavoured soup spiced with the addition of coriander (cilantro). Adding crème fraîche at the end of cooking means the end result is both creamy and tangy on the palate.

celery and leek soup with crème fraîche

SERVES 4–5

1 large head of celery, separated into stalks and chopped
2 leeks, halved lengthways and chopped

1 litre/1¾ pts/4¼ cups water
5 ml/1 tsp ground coriander
Salt and freshly ground black pepper
150 ml/¼ pt/⅔ cup crème fraîche

1 Place all the ingredients except the crème fraîche in a large saucepan and bring gently to the boil.

2 Lower the heat, cover and simmer for 1 hour or until the vegetables are very soft.

3 Blend in two or three batches until smooth, then transfer to a clean saucepan and season with salt and pepper.

4 Stir in the crème fraîche and reheat gently without boiling.

PREPARATION TIME: 15 MINUTES
COOKING TIME: 1¼ HOURS

Excellent as an autumnal dish, this has the tanginess of celery mixed with a slight touch of tartness from the apples. Adding whipping cream at the end of cooking gives the finished result a delicious smoothness, making it great comfort food.

celery and apple soup with pistachio nuts

SERVES 8

2 heads of celery
350 g/12 oz onions, coarsely
   chopped
350 g/12 oz cooking (tart) apples,
   peeled, cored and chopped

1.5 litres/2½ pts/6 cups hot water
Salt and freshly ground black pepper
150 ml/¼ pt/⅔ cup whipping cream
45 ml/3 tbsp pistachio nuts,
   chopped

1 Separate the celery into stalks and slice thinly, including the leaves.

2 Place in a large saucepan with the onions, apples, water, salt and pepper. Bring to the boil.

3 Lower the heat, cover and simmer gently for 1 hour. Leave to cool to lukewarm.

4 Blend half the soup until smooth, then transfer it all to a clean saucepan.

5 Reheat until hot, then gently whisk in the cream.

6 Serve with a sprinkling of nuts on each portion.

PREPARATION TIME: 20 MINUTES
COOKING TIME: 1¼ HOURS

Sunshine in a bowl! This will brighten up any dinner table with its warm and striking colour. If you can't find yellow tomatoes, the recipe will work just as well with red tomatoes.

roasted yellow pepper and yellow tomato soup

SERVES 8

450 g/1 lb yellow (bell) peppers
1 kg/2¼ lb yellow tomatoes,
   blanched, skinned and chopped
175 g/6 oz onions, chopped
1.2 litres/2 pts/5 cups water
10 ml/2 tsp caster (superfine) sugar

5 ml/1 tsp anchovy essence
   (extract)
5 ml/1 tsp Worcestershire sauce

TO SERVE:
Garlic croûtons (page 62)

1   Grill (broil) the peppers all over, turning frequently with tongs, until the skins blister and char to a dark brown colour. Place in a roomy bowl and cover the top closely with clingfilm (plastic wrap).

2   Leave until cold, then rub off the skins under cold running water. Split the peppers and remove the seeds, but save the juices to add to the soup.

3   Place in a large saucepan with all the remaining ingredients and bring to the boil, stirring occasionally.

4   Lower the heat, cover and simmer for 1 hour. Leave to cool to lukewarm.

5   Blend in two or three batches, then transfer to a clean saucepan. Reheat until hot and serve with a topping of the garlic croûtons on each portion.

PREPARATION TIME: 35 MINUTES
COOKING TIME: 1¼ HOURS

Warming and filling, the collection of fresh herbs in this recipe lifts the flavour of the potatoes and gives the soup a wonderful green colour. A generous slice of buttered crusty bread would make a perfect accompaniment.

creamed potato and fresh mixed herb soup

SERVES 5–6

150 g/5 oz fresh parsley
50 g/2 oz fresh flatleaf parsley
50 g/2 oz fresh coriander (cilantro)
 leaves
8 g/¼ oz fresh basil leaves
450 g/1 lb potatoes, peeled and
 cubed

600 ml/1 pt/2½ cups milk
750 ml/1¼ pts/3 cups water
A pinch of salt
150 ml/¼ pt/⅔ cup soured (dairy
 sour) cream

1 Place all the herbs in a large bowl of cold water and leave to soak for at least 1 hour, changing the water twice to remove any grit and dust.

2 Drain and place in a large saucepan with the potatoes, milk, water and salt. Bring gently to the boil.

3 Lower the heat, cover and simmer for 50 minutes. Leave to cool to lukewarm.

4 Blend in two or three batches until smooth, then transfer to a clean saucepan.

5 Add the soured cream and reheat until hot, stirring.

PREPARATION TIME: 10 MINUTES, PLUS SOAKING TIME
COOKING TIME: 1 HOUR

Make the most of cucumbers during the summer months with this mild and attractive soup. Ring the changes by serving with a sprinkling of garlic croûtons or a herb of your choice for some extra flavour instead of the dill.

creamy cucumber and fresh dill soup

SERVES 6–8

900 g/2 lb cucumbers, peeled and
   thinly sliced
30 ml/2 tbsp melted butter
600 ml/1 pt/2½ cups chicken stock

15 ml/1 tbsp cornflour (cornstarch)
450 ml/¾ pt/2 cups milk
45 ml/3 tbsp chopped fresh dill
   (dill weed)

1 Dry the cucumber slices in a clean tea towel (dish cloth), then place in a large saucepan with the butter. Cover and cook over a fairly low heat for 10 minutes.

2 Stir in the stock and bring to the boil.

3 Lower the heat, cover and simmer for 20 minutes. Leave to cool to lukewarm.

4 Blend in two or three batches until smooth, then transfer to a clean saucepan.

5 Mix the cornflour smoothly with a little of the milk, then add to the soup with the remaining milk.

6 Bring to the boil, stirring, then simmer, uncovered, for 5 minutes.

7 Serve with a sprinkling of dill on each portion.

PREPARATION TIME: 10 MINUTES
COOKING TIME: 40 MINUTES

This has a beautiful deep green colour and tastes stunning.
Serve at any time of year, varying the type of salad leaves for
variation. It makes an excellent starter for preceding a light
lunch or supper.

watercress, rocket and spinach soup

SERVES 6

90 g/3½ oz watercress
50 g/2 oz rocket leaves
90 g/3½ oz small spinach leaves
40 g/1½ oz flatleaf parsley
12 shallots, peeled but left whole
15 ml/1 tbsp groundnut (peanut) oil

225 g/8 oz potatoes, peeled and cubed
1.2 litres/2 pts/5 cups vegetable stock
Salt and freshly ground black pepper

1 Place the watercress, rocket, spinach and parsley in a large bowl of cold water and leave to soak for at least 30 minutes, changing the water twice to remove any grit and dust.

2 Fry the shallots in the oil in a large saucepan for about 7 minutes, turning frequently, until golden brown.

3 Add the salad leaves to the pan with the potatoes and stock. Season to taste with salt and pepper. Bring to the boil.

4 Lower the heat, cover and simmer for 30 minutes. Leave to cool to lukewarm.

5 Blend in two or three batches until smooth, then transfer to a clean saucepan.

6 Reheat until very hot before serving.

PREPARATION TIME: 15 MINUTES, PLUS SOAKING TIME
COOKING TIME: 50 MINUTES

MEAT
SOUPS

A fairly substantial group of soups, featuring all varieties of meat including Parma ham, bacon with celeriac (celery root) and carrots, lamb with aubergine (eggplant), ham and split peas, chicken with a Middle Eastern flavour, turkey and root vegetables, game soup with wine, soups from Asia, old-fashioned mulligatawny and even corned beef with potato.

A strong mixture of flavours flows through this warming winter soup. Parma ham is easily obtainable nowadays from most supermarkets but you can easily substitute it, if necessary, with any type of finely sliced cured ham.

celeriac, carrot and leek soup with parma ham

SERVES 8

450 g/l lb celeriac (celery root), diced

225 g/8 oz carrots, diced

3 medium leeks, halved lengthways and sliced

2 litres/3½ pts/8½ cups water

A pinch of salt

15 ml/1 tbsp vegetable stock powder

45 ml/3 tbsp Dijon mustard

60 ml/4 tbsp chopped coriander (cilantro)

100 g/4 oz Parma ham, cut into shreds

1   Place all the ingredients except half the coriander and the Parma ham in a large saucepan and bring to the boil.

2   Lower the heat, cover and simmer gently for 25 minutes or until the vegetables are soft. Leave to cool to lukewarm.

3   Blend in two or three batches until smooth, then transfer to a clean saucepan.

4   Bring gently back to the boil, then serve piping hot, sprinkling each portion with the remaining coriander and the Parma ham shreds.

PREPARATION TIME: 25 MINUTES

COOKING TIME: 45 MINUTES

A very filling soup that makes a hearty meal in itself. It is quite mild flavoured so do experiment by adding different spices to pep things up a bit if you like. Ring the changes by using sweet potatoes or even turnip instead of the celeriac.

celeriac, potato and onion soup with crispy bacon

SERVES 8

225 g/8 oz onions, sliced
30 ml/2 tbsp groundnut (peanut) oil
550 g/1¼ lb potatoes, peeled and cubed
550 g/1¼ lb celeriac (celery root), peeled and cubed
1.5 litres/2½ pts/6 cups water
1.5 ml/¼ tsp grated nutmeg
200 g/7 oz streaky bacon, snipped crossways into strips
45 ml/3 tbsp chopped fresh parsley

1 Fry the onions gently in the oil in a large saucepan for about 10 minutes until lightly golden.

2 Add the potatoes, celeriac, water and nutmeg. Bring to the boil.

3 Lower the heat, cover and simmer gently for 1¼ hours or until the vegetables are soft. Leave to cool to lukewarm.

4 Blend in two or three batches to a coarse purée, then transfer to a clean saucepan.

5 Fry the bacon in its own fat until very crisp.

6 Reheat the soup until hot and serve with the bacon and parsley scattered over each portion.

PREPARATION TIME: 35 MINUTES

COOKING TIME: 1¾ HOURS

The combination of lamb and aubergine is always a winning one and is used to good effect in this delicious dish. There are many varieties of pitta bread available in the supermarkets now so choose an appropriate flavour to complement this tasty soup.

middle eastern-style lamb and aubergine soup

SERVES 6

350 g/12 oz minced (ground) lamb
1 large leek, halved lengthways and sliced
450 g/1 lb aubergine (eggplant), unpeeled and cubed
2 garlic cloves, sliced

900 ml/1½ pts/3¾ cups beef stock
15 ml/1 tbsp malt vinegar
5 ml/1 tsp cornflour (cornstarch)
2.5 ml/½ tsp ground cinnamon
30 ml/2 tbsp lemon juice
45 ml/3 tbsp plain yoghurt

1 Dry-fry the lamb in a heavy-based saucepan for about 7 minutes, stirring frequently, until the grains are browned and separated.

2 Add the leek, aubergine and garlic and fry, turning frequently, until the vegetables begin to brown.

3 Add the stock and bring gently to the boil, stirring occasionally.

4 Mix together the vinegar and cornflour, then add to the soup with the cinnamon and lemon juice. Return to the boil, stirring.

5 Lower the heat, cover and simmer gently for 40 minutes. Leave to cool to lukewarm.

6 Blend in batches until smooth. Cover and chill overnight.

7 Remove any hard layer of fat from the top, then transfer the soup to a saucepan and reheat until just boiling. Serve straight away, topping each portion with a spoonful of yoghurt.

PREPARATION TIME: 30 MINUTES

COOKING TIME: 1 HOUR, PLUS REHEATING

An elegant soup that includes light and nutritious ingredients such as vitamin E packed avocado and sweet asparagus. Combined with beef, they create an earthy flavoured soup with a wonderfully creamy texture. Excellent with brown bread.

creamy avocado and asparagus beef soup

SERVES 4

1 large ripe avocado, halved and stoned (pitted)
300 g/11 oz/1 medium can of condensed beef consommé

375 g/13 oz/1 large jar of green asparagus
600 ml/1 pt/2½ cups water
150 ml/¼ pt/⅔ cup plain yoghurt
4 slices of lemon

1 Scoop the avocado flesh into the blender and add the consommé, the contents of the jar of asparagus and half the water.

2 Blend until smooth, then transfer to a saucepan and gently whisk in the remaining water. Bring just to the boil, stirring.

3 Thoroughly stir in the yoghurt, then spoon into bowls, topping each one with a slice of lemon. Serve straight away.

PREPARATION TIME: 5 MINUTES
COOKING TIME: 5 MINUTES

A highly nutritious soup as yellow split peas are packed with fibre, vitamins and minerals and are low in fat. This rustic style soup is a firm European favourite and is great to have during the cold, wet depths of winter.

yellow split pea and vegetable soup with ham

SERVES 6

225 g/8 oz/1⅓ cups yellow split peas, soaked overnight
1 large ham bone
175 g/6 oz parsnips, chopped
100 g/4 oz carrots, chopped
100 g/4 oz onions, chopped
175 g/6 oz potatoes, peeled and chopped
1.5 litres/2½ pts/6 cups water
1 bay leaf
5–10 ml/1–2 tsp salt
45 ml/3 tbsp chopped fresh parsley

1 Drain the split peas and place in a saucepan with all the remaining ingredients except the parsley.

2 Bring to the boil and boil briskly for 10 minutes.

3 Lower the heat, part-cover and simmer for 1 hour or until the split peas are tender. Leave to cool to lukewarm.

4 Remove and discard the ham bone and bay leaf, picking any remaining meat off the bone and returning it to the saucepan.

5 Reheat until very hot and serve with the parsley sprinkled on each portion.

PREPARATION TIME: 20 MINUTES
COOKING TIME: 1¼ HOURS

Packed with health-giving vegetables, this soup also makes excellent use of chicken wings. It's easy to adapt this recipe to suit the seasons so try experimenting with as many different vegetables as you like.

middle eastern chicken and vegetable soup

SERVES 4

75 g/3 oz carrots, cubed
100 g/4 oz potatoes, peeled and cubed
75 g/3 oz parsnips, cubed
100 g/4 oz onions, sliced
1 celery stalk, sliced
100 g/4 oz marrow (squash) or pumpkin (prepared weight)

90 ml/1½ pts/3¾ cups chicken stock
30 ml/2 tbsp barley
15 ml/1 tbsp porridge oats
Salt and freshly ground black pepper
8 chicken wings

1 Place all the ingredients except the chicken wings in a large saucepan and bring to the boil.

2 Lower the heat, cover and simmer gently for 30 minutes.

3 Add the chicken wings and continue to cook for a further 20 minutes or until the vegetables are soft.

4 Remove the wings and set aside. Leave the soup to cool to lukewarm.

5 Blend in two or three batches to a coarse purée, then transfer to a clean saucepan.

6 Return the wings to the soup and reheat gently, stirring from time to time, until very hot.

7 Serve straight away, making sure each portion has a chicken wing.

PREPARATION TIME: 15 MINUTES
COOKING TIME: 1 HOUR

This is a light and elegant soup that makes an excellent starter at any time of the year. The soup itself is not green but the attractive garnish of chives added just before serving is what gives this soup its name.

swiss-style creamy green onion soup

SERVES 6

450 g/1 lb onions, sliced
60 ml/4 tbsp melted butter
5 ml/1 tsp olive oil
20 ml/4 tsp plain (all-purpose) flour

900 ml/1½ pts/3¾ cups hot chicken
   or beef stock
150 ml/¼ pt/⅔ cup whipping cream
90 ml/6 tbsp snipped fresh chives

1   Place the onions in a saucepan with the butter and oil. Part-cover and fry very gently for about 20 minutes until the onions begin to soften but do not allow to brown.

2   Stir in the flour and cook for 1 minute, then gradually work in the stock and bring gently to the boil, stirring.

3   Lower the heat, cover and simmer gently for 25 minutes, stirring from time to time. Leave to cool to lukewarm.

4   Blend in two or three batches until smooth, then transfer to a clean saucepan.

5   Gently whisk in the cream and reheat until hot without boiling.

6   Serve straight away, with a sprinkling of chives on each portion.

PREPARATION TIME: 20 MINUTES
COOKING TIME: 50 MINUTES

This is ideal after Christmas when there is a turkey carcass to be made use of. The recipe creates a cheerful, heartening soup that makes a lovely main meal, especially when served with copious amounts of brown bread sandwiches and coleslaw.

turkey soup with lemon, tarragon and thyme

SERVES 6–8

100 g/4 oz carrots, cut into chunks
100 g/4 oz potatoes, cut into chunks
100 g/4 oz swede (rutabaga) or parsnip, cut into chunks
175 g/6 oz onions, cut into chunks
1 large leek, sliced
45 ml/3 tbsp brown rice

1 turkey carcass, broken into pieces
1.75 litres/3 pts/7½ cups water
15 ml/1 tbsp chopped tarragon
2 whole garlic cloves
10 ml/2 tsp finely grated lemon rind
5 ml/1 tsp dried thyme
45–60 ml/3–4 tbsp melted butter

1 Place all the ingredients except the melted butter in a large saucepan. Bring gently to the boil.

2 Lower the heat, cover and simmer gently for 1¼ hours.

3 Remove the carcass, take off any pieces of meat and stuffing still remaining and return to the pan. Discard the bones. Leave the soup to cool to lukewarm.

4 Blend in three or four batches until semi-smooth, then transfer to a clean saucepan.

5 Reheat until very hot, then serve with a drizzle of melted butter on each portion.

PREPARATION TIME: 30 MINUTES
COOKING TIME: 1½ HOURS

Another good way of using up a chicken carcass, this traditional soup makes the most of spare vegetables and storecupboard ingredients. For variation, try using tapioca or couscous instead of barley to bulk out the soup.

country-style chicken broth with barley and sage

SERVES 6–8

1 chicken carcass, broken into pieces
1.5 litres/2½ pts/6 cups beef stock
40 g/1½ oz barley
2 celery sticks, sliced

1 leek, halved lengthways and sliced
225 g/8 oz carrots, sliced
225 g/8 oz cauliflower florets
5 ml/1 tsp dried sage
30–45 ml/2–3 tbsp dried fried onions

1 Place the carcass in a large saucepan with the stock and barley. Bring gently to the boil.

2 Add the remaining ingredients except the fried onions, mix well and return to the boil.

3 Lower the heat, cover and simmer gently for 1¼ hours.

4 Remove the carcass, take off any pieces of meat and stuffing still remaining and return to the pan. Discard the bones. Leave the soup to cool to lukewarm.

5 Blend in three or four batches until semi-smooth, then transfer to a clean saucepan.

6 Reheat the soup until very hot and serve with a sprinkling of the dried onions on each portion.

PREPARATION TIME: 30 MINUTES

COOKING TIME: 1½ HOURS

There are a multitude of flavours running through this soup, with the fennel adding an unusual anise taste to the chicken and vegetables. Tapioca helps to thicken the soup but you can use white rice instead, if preferred.

chicken soup with carrot, fennel and tapioca

SERVES 4

30 ml/2 tbsp tapioca
1 leg and thigh chicken joint, about 225 g/8 oz
175 g/6 oz onions, coarsely chopped
2 celery stalks, sliced

1 head of fennel, about 225 g/8 oz, sliced
15 g/½ oz parsley
900 ml/1½ pts/3¾ cups water
300 ml/½ pt/1¼ cups carrot juice
Salt and freshly ground black pepper

1 Soak the tapioca in enough water to cover for a minimum of 1 hour.

2 Place the remaining ingredients in a large saucepan and bring to the boil, stirring.

3 Lower the heat, cover and simmer gently for 1 hour.

4 Remove the chicken joint and leave the soup to cool to lukewarm.

5 Take the meat off the chicken joint and shred with two forks. Set aside.

6 Blend the soup in two or three batches to a coarse purée, then transfer to a clean saucepan.

7 Add the tapioca and soaking water to the pan and bring to the boil. Lower the heat, add the chicken shreds and simmer for 10 minutes.

8 Serve very hot.

PREPARATION TIME: 15 MINUTES, PLUS SOAKING TIME
COOKING TIME: 1¼ HOURS

Using a variety of spices and herbs, this is a richly flavoured soup. The addition of rice and lentils ensures the end result is exotic, filling and delicious. Add more yoghurt if required and serve with warmed naan or keema naan breads.

asian chicken soup with basmati rice and lentils

SERVES 4

1 leg and thigh chicken joint, about 225 g/8 oz
175 g/6 oz onions, coarsely chopped
1 green chilli, slit and seeds removed
2–3 garlic cloves, thinly sliced
25 g/1 oz fresh root ginger, thinly sliced
25 g/1 oz coriander (cilantro) leaves

10 ml/2 tsp garam masala
5 ml/1 tsp ground cumin
2.5 ml/½ tsp ground turmeric
2.5 ml/½ tsp ground coriander
45 ml/3 tbsp orange lentils
30 ml/2 tbsp basmati rice
1.2 litres/2 pts/5 cups water
150 ml/¼ pt/⅔ cup plain yoghurt

TO SERVE:
Naan breads

1 Place the chicken, onions, chilli, garlic, ginger and coriander leaves in a large saucepan.

2 Sprinkle the garam masala, cumin, turmeric and ground coriander over the chicken and vegetables, then mix in the lentils and rice.

3 Add the water and bring to the boil, stirring.

4 Lower the heat, cover and simmer gently for 1 hour.

5 Remove the chicken joint and leave the soup to cool to lukewarm. Take the meat off the chicken joint and cut into strips. Set aside.

6 Blend the soup in two or three batches to a coarse purée, then transfer to a clean saucepan. Bring to the boil, stirring.

7 Add the chicken strips and simmer for 10 minutes.

8 Stir in the yoghurt and serve very hot with naan breads.

PREPARATION TIME: 30 MINUTES
COOKING TIME: 1¾ HOURS

An interesting combination of traditional English and African ingredients that creates another very filling soup that would make an ideal main meal. If you are pushed for time, you can substitute the fresh cabbage with shredded frozen cabbage.

couscous and cabbage soup with sausages

SERVES 6

450 g/1 lb green cabbage, shredded
45 ml/3 tbsp couscous
1.5 litres/2½ pts/6 cups water
5 ml/1 tsp wholegrain mustard

1.5 ml/¼ tsp ground allspice
5 ml/1 tsp salt
450 g/1 lb cooked pork sausages,
    diagonally sliced

1 Place all the ingredients except the sausages in a large saucepan. Bring to the boil.

2 Lower the heat, cover and simmer for 40 minutes, stirring occasionally. Leave to cool to lukewarm.

3 Blend in two or three batches to a coarse purée, then transfer to a clean saucepan.

4 Add the sausage slices and reheat until very hot.

PREPARATION TIME: 10 MINUTES
COOKING TIME: 50 MINUTES

Don't be put off by the long list of ingredients for this recipe. The end result is worth the effort and gives you a deep orange soup flavoured with Indian spices and topped with cooling yoghurt and refreshing cucumber. Serve with naan bread.

tandoori lamb soup
with yoghurt and cucumber

SERVES 6

20 ml/4 tsp groundnut (peanut) oil
175 g/6 oz onions, coarsely
  chopped
2 garlic cloves, thinly sliced
1 red (bell) pepper, seeded and
  coarsely chopped
100 g/4 oz fresh spinach leaves,
  torn into small pieces
225 g/8 oz minced (ground) lamb
30 ml/2 tbsp tandoori spice mix
5 ml/1 tsp ground cardamom

2.5 ml/½ tsp ground ginger
1.5 ml/¼ tsp ground allspice
30 ml/2 tbsp chutney
45 ml/3 tbsp chopped coriander
  (cilantro)
30 ml/2 tbsp tomato purée (paste)
1.5 litres/2½ pts/6 cups water
Salt and freshly ground black pepper
30 ml/2 tbsp plain yoghurt
30 ml/2 tbsp shredded cucumber

1 Heat the oil in a large saucepan until sizzling.

2 Add the onions, garlic, chopped pepper and spinach and fry (sauté) gently for 10 minutes or until the vegetables are just beginning to turn golden.

3 Mix in the lamb and cook, stirring often, until the grains of lamb are browned and separated. Continue cooking for a further 10 minutes.

4 Add all the spices, then the chutney, coriander, tomato purée, water, salt and pepper. Bring to the boil, stirring.

5 Lower the heat, cover and simmer gently for 1 hour, stirring occasionally. Leave to cool, then chill for about 12 hours.

6 Remove any hard layer of fat from the surface, then blend the soup in two or three batches to a coarse purée.

7 Transfer to a clean saucepan and reheat until very hot.

8 Serve each portion topped with the yoghurt and cucumber.

PREPARATION TIME: 30 MINUTES

COOKING TIME: 1 ½ HOURS

A Far-Eastern inspired broth combining an exotic mixture of spices with succulent chicken breast. If you are unable to buy red imperial rice, any form of white rice will make an adequate substitute. Excellent served as a starter to a Chinese meal.

imperial chinese chicken and red rice soup

SERVES 4

350 g/12 oz onions, coarsely chopped
25 g/1 oz fresh root ginger, coarsely chopped
2 celery stalks, sliced
225 g/8 oz boned chicken breast
30 ml/2 tbsp low-salt soy sauce
15 ml/1 tbsp mushroom ketchup (catsup)

5 ml/1 tsp five-spice powder
45 ml/3 tbsp red imperial rice
1.2 litres/2 pts/5 cups water
A pinch of salt
30 ml/2 tbsp lemon juice
5–20 ml/1–4 tsp chilli sauce
100 g/4 oz/2 cups beansprouts

1 Place all the ingredients except the lemon juice, chilli sauce and beansprouts in a large saucepan. Bring to the boil, stirring.

2 Lower the heat, cover and simmer gently for 1 hour.

3 Remove the chicken breast and leave the soup to cool to lukewarm. Cut the meat into small cubes.

4 Blend the soup in two or three batches to a coarse purée, then transfer to a clean saucepan.

5 Add the lemon juice and chilli sauce to taste and bring to the boil. Lower the heat and simmer for 5 minutes.

6 Add the chicken cubes and beansprouts and reheat for 5 minutes.

7 Serve very hot.

PREPARATION TIME: 25 MINUTES
COOKING TIME: 1½ HOURS

Kidneys are very high in protein yet they are low in fat, which makes them ideal for those who are watching their weight. This soup makes sophisticated use of lambs' kidneys and the end result is a nutritional and tasty soup.

traditional
lambs' kidney soup

SERVES 4

250 g/9 oz lambs' kidneys
175 g/6 oz onions, thinly sliced
15 ml/1 tbsp groundnut (peanut) oil
600 ml/1 pt/2½ cups water
5 ml/1 tsp salt
15 ml/1 tbsp plain (all-purpose) flour
450 ml/¾ pt/2 cups dry red wine

15 ml/1 tbsp redcurrant jelly (clear conserve)
10 ml/2 tsp Worcestershire sauce
4 ml/¾ tsp made English mustard

TO SERVE:
Cheese straws or biscuits (crackers)

1 Wash and slice the kidneys, removing excess fat from the centre of each slice.

2 Gently fry (sauté) the onions in the oil in a saucepan for about 12 minutes until a warm golden brown.

3 Add the kidneys and fry for 10 minutes.

4 Add the water and salt and bring gently to the boil.

5 Lower the heat, cover and simmer gently for 40 minutes, stirring occasionally. Leave to cool to lukewarm. Add the flour.

6 Blend until fairly smooth and return to the saucepan. Add the wine, redcurrant jelly, Worcestershire sauce and mustard.

7 Cook, stirring, until the soup comes to the boil and thickens. Simmer for 5 minutes.

8 Serve each portion accompanied by a cheese straw or biscuit.

PREPARATION TIME: 25 MINUTES
COOKING TIME: 1¼ HOURS

This is a treat to make as venison can be a bit expensive. It is low in fat and high in protein, vitamin B, iron, potassium and phosphorus. Combined with the vegetables in this recipe, this is a healthy soup tastefully seasoned with aromatic juniper berries.

game soup with wine, cream and orange

SERVES 8

30 ml/2 tbsp sunflower oil
100 g/4 oz onions, cut into small cubes
100 g/4 oz carrots, cut into small cubes
225 g/8 oz potatoes, peeled and cut into small cubes
175 g/6 oz venison steak
225 g/8 oz tomatoes, blanched, skinned and coarsely chopped

750 ml/1¼ pts/3 cups beef stock
300 ml/½ pt/1¼ cups red wine
15 ml/1 tbsp tomato purée (paste)
10 ml/2 tsp brown sugar
10 ml/2 tsp lemon juice
6 juniper berries, crushed
A pinch of salt
150 ml/¼ pt/⅔ cup single (light) cream
Finely grated orange rind, to garnish

1 Heat the oil in a large saucepan until sizzling.

2 Add the onions, carrots and potatoes and fry (sauté) gently, part-covered, for 10 minutes.

3 Add the venison and fry for 6 minutes, turning twice.

4 Add the tomatoes and fry for 5 minutes.

5 Thoroughly mix in the stock, wine, tomato purée, sugar, lemon juice, juniper berries and salt. Bring gently to the boil.

6 Lower the heat, cover and simmer for 45 minutes or until the vegetables are tender.

7 Lift out the venison and cut into narrow strips. Leave the soup to cool to lukewarm.

8 Blend the soup in two or three batches until smooth, then transfer to a clean saucepan.

9   Add the venison and reheat the soup until very hot. Stir in the cream.

10 Serve with a sprinkling of orange rind on each portion.

PREPARATION TIME: 40 MINUTES

COOKING TIME: 1¼ HOURS

This is based on a traditional South African recipe and makes a fulfilling winter meal full of soluble fibre and nutrients. Make sure you do boil the dried beans as directed in step 1 as this is necessary to destroy any toxins.

butter bean and bacon soup

SERVES 6

225 g/8 oz/1⅓ cups dried butter (lima) beans, soaked overnight
1.5 litres/2½ pts/6 cups beef stock
175 g/6 oz onions, cubed
350 g/12 oz potatoes, peeled and cubed

175 g/6 oz tomatoes, blanched, skinned and coarsely chopped
2 back bacon rashers (slices), trimmed and cut into strips
5 ml/1 tsp chopped fresh parsley

1 Drain the beans and place in a large saucepan with the stock. Bring to the boil and boil briskly for 10 minutes.

2 Add the onions, potatoes, tomatoes and bacon and return to the boil.

3 Lower the heat, cover and simmer for 1 hour. Leave to cool to lukewarm.

4 Blend in two or three batches to a coarse purée, then transfer to a clean saucepan.

5 Before serving, reheat the soup to piping hot and sprinkle each portion with the parsley.

PREPARATION TIME: 20 MINUTES
COOKING TIME: 1¼ HOURS

Mulligatawny means 'pepper water' and rumour has it that in the days of the Raj, the English adapted a traditional spiced pea and lentil Indian dish to suit their taste for soup. Try adding coconut milk or cream instead of yoghurt for an exotic change.

mulligatawny soup

SERVES 6

30 ml/2 tbsp groundnut (peanut) oil
175 g/6 oz carrots, sliced
175 g/6 oz onions, sliced
2 celery stalks, cut into short
   lengths
25 g/1 oz/¼ cup plain (all purpose)
   flour
15 ml/1 tbsp Madras curry powder
1 litre/1¾ pts/4¼ cups hot beef
   stock

175 g/6 oz cooking (tart) apples,
   peeled, cored and coarsely
   chopped
30 ml/2 tbsp raisins
30 ml/2 tbsp lemon juice
10 ml/2 tsp brown sugar
75 g/3 oz/¾ cup cooked chicken,
   cut into narrow strips
90 g/3½ oz/7 tbsp cooked rice
45 ml/3 tbsp plain yoghurt

1 Heat the oil in a large saucepan until sizzling. Add the carrots, onions and celery and fry (sauté) until lightly golden. Stir in the flour and curry powder and cook for 2 minutes.

2 Blend in the hot stock a little at a time, then cook, stirring, until the mixture comes to the boil and thickens.

3 Add the apples, raisins, lemon juice and sugar and return to the boil. Lower the heat, cover and simmer gently for 1 hour, stirring fairly often to prevent sticking. Leave to cool to lukewarm.

4 Blend in two or three batches until smooth, then transfer to a clean saucepan. Reheat gently until hot.

5 Divide the chicken strips and rice equally between warm soup bowls and top up with hot soup. Add a spoonful of yoghurt to each and serve.

PREPARATION TIME: 30 MINUTES
COOKING TIME: 1¼ HOURS

Cheap and tasty, this thick and filling soup is ideal for a quick and easy supper for the family. If you have more time, use freshly boiled potatoes instead of the canned. Serve with plenty of sliced, buttered bread.

quick corned beef and potato soup

SERVES 4–6

340 g/12 oz/1 medium can of
   corned beef
545 g/1¼ lb/1 very large can of
   potatoes in water or brine
600 ml/1 pt/2½ cups water

10 ml/2 tsp made English mustard
30 ml/2 tbsp brown ketchup
   (catsup)
Salt and freshly ground black pepper
90 ml/6 tbsp chopped parsley

1   Halve the block of corned beef. Coarsely mash one half and cut the other into small pieces.

2   Drain the potatoes, reserving the liquid. Cut the potatoes into small pieces.

3   Place in the blender with the reserved liquid and half the water. Blend until fairly smooth and pour into a saucepan.

4   Stir in the remaining water, the mashed corned beef, the mustard and ketchup and season with a little salt and generously with pepper. Bring to the boil, stirring all the time.

5   Lower the heat and simmer for 5 minutes.

6   Add the remaining corned beef and mix in thoroughly.

7   Serve very hot and shower each portion heavily with the parsley.

PREPARATION TIME: 10 MINUTES

COOKING TIME: 10 MINUTES

SEAFOOD
SOUPS

Because fish soup is less familiar in Britain than in its European neighbours and other countries even further afield, the selection in this chapter has focused on speciality soups with gourmet appeal from the Far East and France.

More a chowder fish meal than just a soup, laksa is a fish stock with seasonings and coconut milk, afloat with rice vermicelli, seafood, vegetables and sometimes fruit. A Malaysian speciality – with no two versions alike – it is sold by street hawkers in the Far East and also made at home by dedicated cooks. Its preparation is long but the end result is a delicious and memorable eating experience. It is a dramatic favourite with the 'smart set' from India to Thailand to China, brilliant for entertaining if you only want a one-dish meal. Start with the additions, which can be made early on and left, covered and chilled, until the laksa is ready to be served.

penang laksa

SERVES 6

ADDITIONS:
1 small lettuce, shredded
¼ cucumber, unpeeled and diced
6 spring onions (scallions), thinly
    sliced
10 mint leaves, cut into strips
A 2.5 cm/1 in slice of fresh
    pineapple, cut into small pieces
90 ml/6 tbsp beansprouts
400 g/14 oz frozen king prawns
    (jumbo shrimp), defrosted as
    directed on the packet

FOR THE LAKSA:
2 stalks of lemon grass, cut into
    short lengths

2 garlic cloves, halved
A walnut-sized piece of fresh root
    ginger, sliced
1 onion, sliced
8 macadamia nuts or blanched
    almonds
2 large sun-dried red chillies
30 ml/2 tbsp chopped coriander
    (cilantro)
5 ml/1 tsp ground turmeric
15 ml/1 tbsp fish sauce
400 ml/14 fl oz/1¾ cups canned
    coconut milk
1.2 litres/2 pts/5 cups well-flavoured
    fish stock
250 g/9 oz rice vermicelli

1   Arrange the additions attractively on a large plate, keeping each one separate. Cover with clingfilm (plastic wrap) and chill until ready to serve.

2   To make the laksa, place the lemon grass, garlic, ginger, onion, nuts, chillies, a quarter of the coriander, the turmeric, fish sauce and coconut milk in a blender and blend until smooth.

3   Transfer to a large saucepan and add the fish stock. Bring to the boil.

4   Meanwhile, soak the vermicelli in boiling water for 5 minutes. Drain and divide between six large, deep soup bowls. Sprinkle with the prawns and other additions, then top up with the boiling stock.

5   Sprinkle heavily with the remaining coriander and serve straight away.

Notes:

1   For convenience, you could substitute fish stock cubes and water for the fish stock and canned pineapple for fresh.

2   As a variation, use cooked and flaked salmon or salmon trout, or any other cooked and flaked white fish, instead of the prawns.

3   For a hotter soup, increase the chillies to a maximum of eight.

PREPARATION TIME: 1–1¼ HOURS
COOKING TIME: 15 MINUTES

The star attraction of the show and a glittering performer, this is soup at its very finest: a soft and smooth blend of assorted fish and vegetables simmered in fish stock with saffron to give a note of exclusivity. Particular to the South of France, the soup has been lovingly developed over many years by the international restaurant fraternity and, should you be eating out and order a fish soup, there is a strong possibility that it will closely resemble the one given here. Rouille, a traditional and fairly fiery condiment, is stirred into each portion at the table to further enrich and enliven the flavour.

classic fish soup

SERVES 8

FOR THE SOUP:
1.5–2.5 ml/¼–½ tsp saffron strands
15 ml/1 tbsp hot water
250 g/9 oz onions, very thinly sliced
2 garlic cloves, very thinly sliced
1 celery stick, very thinly sliced
25 ml/1½ tbsp olive or groundnut (peanut) oil
450 g/1 lb tomatoes, blanched, skinned and coarsely chopped
30 ml/2 tbsp tomato purée (paste)
350 g/12 oz hake or haddock fillet, skinned and cubed
450 g/1 lb salmon fillet, skinned and cubed

1.5 litres/2½ pts/6 cups cold water
300 ml/½ pt/1¼ cups dry white wine

FOR THE ROUILLE:
75 g/3 oz bread slices with crusts, cubed
1 red chilli, about 50 g/2 oz, halved and seeded
3 garlic cloves
30 ml/2 tbsp tomato purée (paste)
45 ml/3 tbsp olive oil
30 ml/2 tbsp boiling water
2.5 ml/½ tsp salt

TO SERVE:
Baguette slices

1 To make the soup, soak the saffron in the hot water in a small basin for a minimum of 30 minutes.

2 Place the onions, garlic and celery in a saucepan with the oil and fry for 5–6 minutes until they are just beginning to turn lightly golden.

3 Add the remaining ingredients, including the saffron and soaking water. Bring to the boil,

4 Lower the heat, cover and simmer gently for 45 minutes, stirring once or twice. Leave to cool to lukewarm.

5 To make the rouille, place all the ingredients in the blender and blend to form a smooth paste.

6 Blend the soup in two or three batches until smooth, then transfer to a clean saucepan.

7 Reheat until very hot before serving with a side dish of rouille and slices of baguette.

Notes:

1 An easier rouille can be made by mixing 90 ml/6 tbsp thick mayonnaise with 2 peeled and crushed garlic cloves and 30 ml/2 tbsp chilli sauce.

2 After blending, the rouille can be packed into a screw-topped jar, the top smoothed and then coated with extra oil, and stored for up to 10 days. Stir before serving.

PREPARATION TIME: 40 MINUTES FOR THE SOUP, PLUS SOAKING
TIME; 15 MINUTES FOR THE ROUILLE
COOKING TIME: 1 HOUR

crab bisque

SERVES 8

Prepare as for Classic Fish Soup, but after reheating stir in 200 g/ 7 oz cooked crab meat (fresh or canned), 150 ml/¼ pt/⅔ cup single (light) cream and 15 ml/1 tbsp brandy. Serve hot, with or without the rouille.

An aromatic blend of the Far-East that creates a creamy, fragrant soup. This soup is quick to assemble and put together and can be left to simmer on its own quite easily. You can ring the changes by substituting a different meat to pork.

thai rice cream soup with lime, lemon grass and prawns

SERVES 6

1 stick of lemon grass, chopped
3 lime leaves
Juice of 1 lime
A 5 cm/2 in whole green chilli
4 garlic cloves
175 g/6 oz pork fillet, cut into strips
90 g/3½ oz/scant ½ cup Thai fragrant rice

400 g/14 oz/1 large can of coconut milk
1.5 litres/2½ pts/6 cups chicken stock
25 g/1 oz coriander (cilantro) leaves
350 g/12 oz cooked, peeled prawns (shrimp)

1   Place all the ingredients except half the coriander and the prawns in a large saucepan. Bring to the boil.

2   Lower the heat, cover and simmer for 1 hour, stirring occasionally.

3   Leave to cool to lukewarm. Remove and discard the lime leaves.

4   Blend in two or three batches until fairly smooth, then transfer to a clean saucepan.

5   Reheat until hot, then add the prawns and warm through for 2 minutes.

6   Finely chop the remaining coriander and sprinkle over the soup to serve.

PREPARATION TIME: 15 MINUTES

COOKING TIME: 1¼ HOURS

This has all the flavour of the other fish soups covered in this chapter but has been especially created for slimmers. This recipe is easily adapted to suit all tastes so experiment and try other canned seafood such as crab for a tasty alternative to tuna.

speedy tuna and tomato soup

SERVES 4–6

2 × 185 g/2 × 6½ oz/2 small cans
of tuna in brine
400 g/14 oz/1 large can of chopped
tomatoes
30 ml/2 tbsp capers
2 garlic cloves, crushed
150 ml/¼ pt/⅔ cup dry white wine
30 ml/2 tbsp anchovy essence
(extract)

10 ml/2 tsp cornflour (cornstarch)
15 ml/1 tbsp water
15–30 ml/1–2 tbsp chilli purée
(paste)
15 ml/1 tbsp sun-dried tomato
purée
Salt and freshly ground black pepper

1 Tip the contents of the cans of tuna into the blender. Add the tomatoes, capers, garlic, wine and anchovy essence. Blend until very smooth and pour into a saucepan.

2 Mix the cornflour smoothly with the water and add to the pan with the chilli and tomato purées.

3 Bring to the boil, stirring, then taste and season with a little salt and pepper if necessary. Simmer gently for 4 minutes.

4 Serve very hot and, if liked, accompany with rouille (pages 102–3).

PREPARATION TIME: 10 MINUTES
COOKING TIME: 10 MINUTES

A variation of 'Cullen Skink'; a hearty fish and potato soup derived from the north-east of Scotland, namely the coastal region of Cullen on the Moray Firth. This soup has a wonderful smooth texture with a distinct smokiness from the haddock.

smoked haddock cream soup with potatoes and onions

SERVES 6

700 g/1½ lb potatoes, peeled and cubed
175 g/6 oz onions, thinly sliced
1.2 litres/2 pts/5 cups water
A pinch of salt

450 g/1 lb smoked haddock fillet, skinned and cut into squares
90 ml/6 tbsp whipping cream
60 ml/4 tbsp chopped fresh parsley

1 Place the potatoes and onions in a saucepan with the water and salt. Bring to the boil.

2 Lower the heat, cover and simmer for 40 minutes until the vegetables are very soft. Leave to cool to lukewarm.

3 Blend in two or three batches until smooth, then transfer to a clean saucepan.

4 Add the haddock and return the soup to the boil. Simmer for 2 minutes.

5 Remove from the heat and stir in the cream.

6 Serve very hot with a sprinkling of parsley on each portion.

PREPARATION TIME: 15 MINUTES
COOKING TIME: 50 MINUTES

SMOOTHIES

Smoothies look something like thinned-down milkshakes in assorted colours — some dark, others light — and give spectacular flavour bursts of various fruits when they are sweet, or of mixed vegetables when savoury. They are a hugely popular way to get your daily intake of fruit and vegetables as they provide refreshing and nourishing drinks right through the year. They are also easy to make and, in some cases, purer and more economical than bought smoothies.

A mild tasting smoothie packed with banana enriched vitamins and minerals. Excellent for a tea-time treat or as a dessert. Try grating some high-quality chocolate on top of the smoothie before serving for an attractive finish.

banana and caramel smoothie

SERVES 4

4 bananas, peeled
30 ml/2 tbsp caramel-flavoured
  syrup

10 ml/2 tsp grated orange rind
600 ml/1 pt/2½ cups full cream milk

1   Break the banana flesh into the blender and add the remaining ingredients. Blend until smooth. Pour into a bowl or jug, cover and chill thoroughly.

2   Stir before serving in glasses or mugs.

PREPARATION TIME: 10 MINUTES

An exotic smoothie, perfect for serving on a warm summer's day. If you are pushed for time, you can use a large can of pineapple chunks instead of peeling and cubing a fresh fruit. Add copious amounts of ice cubes for a refreshing drink.

pineapple, lime and apple smoothie

SERVES 4

1 large eating (dessert) apple,
  peeled, cored and quartered
½ large pineapple, peeled and flesh
  cubed
Juice of 1 lime

150 ml/¼ pt/⅔ cup water
300 ml/½ pt/1¼ cups tropical-style
  fruit juice
4 fresh mint leaves

1   Cut the apple quarters into cubes and place in the blender with the remaining ingredients. Blend until smooth. Pour into a bowl or jug, cover and chill thoroughly.

2   Stir before serving in glasses or mugs.

PREPARATION TIME: 10 MINUTES

Strawberries are a major type of superfood, packed with anti-oxidants and flavonoids. This smoothie uses plenty of strawberries and ensures that as well as providing a deliciously fruity taste, the smoothie is full of nutritional goodness too.

strawberry and orangeade smoothie

SERVES 4

450 g/1 lb fresh strawberries, hulled
300 ml/½ pt/1¼ cups strawberry-flavoured yoghurt

350 ml/12 fl oz/1⅓ cups orangeade, chilled

1   Place the strawberries and yoghurt in the blender and blend until smooth. Pour into a bowl or jug, cover and chill thoroughly.

2   Stir in the orangeade before serving in glasses or mugs.

PREPARATION TIME: 6 MINUTES

Make the most of the summery fruits on offer with this delicious smoothie that has been given an adult twist with a dash of red wine. Try serving in glasses filled with ice cubes and decorated with sliced fruit.

strawberry, orange and pineapple smoothie

SERVES 4–5

1 orange, peeled
450 g/1 lb strawberries, hulled

450 ml/¾ pt/2 cups pineapple juice
150 ml/¼ pt/⅔ cup red wine

1   Separate the orange into segments and remove the pips. Place in the blender with the strawberries and half the pineapple juice. Blend until smooth.

2   Pour into a bowl or jug, then stir in the remaining pineapple juice and the wine. Cover and chill thoroughly. Stir before serving in glasses or mugs.

PREPARATION TIME: 10 MINUTES

There is an interesting mix of flavours in this smoothie but it is quite delicious. Try to use a good-quality vanilla ice cream as this will ensure that the end result is creamy and full of flavour.

strawberry and peach smoothie with vanilla ice and rose water

SERVES 5–6

450 g/1 lb strawberries, hulled
450 ml/¾ pt/2 cups peach juice

250 ml/8 fl oz/1 cup vanilla ice
   cream
15 ml/1 tbsp rose water

1 Place the strawberries in the blender with half the peach juice, the ice cream and rose water. Blend until smooth.

2 Pour into a bowl and add the remaining peach juice. Cover and chill for several hours.

3 Stir before serving in glasses or mugs.

PREPARATION TIME: 6 MINUTES

An unusual smoothie that has a beautiful colour, speckled with blueberry seeds. Custard apples are also called sour sop or guanabana and have a distinctive taste. If you are unable to obtain them, try persimmon as it is a very sweet fruit when ripe.

nectarine, blueberry and custard apple juice smoothie

SERVES 4–6

3 ripe nectarines, halved and stoned (pitted)
250 g/9 oz blueberries

600 ml/1 pt/2½ cups custard apple juice

1 Cut the nectarine halves into chunks and place in the blender with the blueberries and half the apple juice. Blend until smooth.

2 Pour into a bowl and stir in the remaining apple juice. Cover and chill for several hours.

3 Stir before serving in glasses or mugs.

PREPARATION TIME: 5 MINUTES

A lightly perfumed drink that tastes delicious. For best results, make sure the raspberries are in season and ripe. For a subtle change in flavour, try experimenting with different types of honey, such as blossom, manuka or acacia.

raspberry, banana and pink grapefruit smoothie

SERVES 4–5

2 bananas, peeled
225 g/8 oz raspberries

30 ml/2 tbsp thick honey
600 ml/1 pt/2½ cups pink grapefruit juice

1 Break the banana flesh into the blender and add the raspberries, honey and half the grapefruit juice. Blend until smooth.

2 Pour into a bowl or jug and stir in the remaining grapefruit juice. Cover and chill thoroughly.

3 Stir before serving in glasses or mugs.

PREPARATION TIME: 5 MINUTES

An exotic and refreshing smoothie dominated by the sweet tangy flavour of mango. Mangoes are high in iron, potassium and magnesium which makes this delicious drink beneficial for those suffering from anaemia, muscle cramps and heart problems.

mango, mandarin orange and lemonade smoothie

SERVES 3–4

2 ripe mangoes
300 g/11 oz/1 medium can of
   mandarin oranges in light syrup

300 ml/½ pt/1¼ cups lemonade

1 Peel the mangoes and cut the flesh away from the stones (pits).

2 Transfer the flesh to the blender and add the contents of the can of mandarins and half the lemonade. Blend until smooth.

3 Pour into a bowl or jug and stir in the remaining lemonade. Cover and chill thoroughly.

4 Stir before serving in glasses or mugs.

PREPARATION TIME: 5 MINUTES

Traditional flavours abound in this old-fashioned smoothie that gives a wonderful fragrance and tastes great. Try to use organic, fresh rhubarb as this will intensify the flavours. The end result is quite sweet and would make an unusual dessert.

rhubarb and custard smoothie with elderflower

SERVES 4–5

450 g/1 lb rhubarb, cut into pieces
300 ml/½ pt/1¼ cups water
60 ml/4 tbsp elderflower cordial

600 ml/1 pt/2½ cups sparkling elderflower drink
300 ml/½ pt/1¼ cups sweetened custard sauce

1   Place the rhubarb in a saucepan with the water. Cover and cook for 8 minutes or until the rhubarb is soft and pulpy. Leave to cool.

2   Transfer the rhubarb and cooking water to the blender. Add the elderflower cordial and half the elderflower drink and blend until smooth.

3   Pour into a bowl or jug and stir in the remaining elderflower drink and the custard sauce. Cover and chill thoroughly.

4   Stir before serving in glasses or mugs.

PREPARATION TIME: 10 MINUTES
COOKING TIME: 10 MINUTES

This is ideal for giving yourself a nutritional boost during the autumn (fall) season. If you don't have a microwave, the plums and marmalade can be easily heated on the hob. Try experimenting with different varieties of plum.

plum, marmalade and apple smoothie

SERVES 6

700 g/1½ lb firm golden plums, halved and stoned (pitted)

200 g/7 oz/generous ½ cup coarse-cut dark orange marmalade

900 ml/1½ pts/3¾ cups apple juice

1 Place the plums in a glass dish and stir in the marmalade. Microwave, uncovered, on full power for 8–10 minutes, stirring several times until tender. Leave to cool to lukewarm.

2 Transfer to the blender and add half the apple juice. Blend until smooth. Pour into a bowl or jug and stir in the remaining apple juice. Cover and chill thoroughly. Stir before serving in glasses or mugs.

PREPARATION TIME: 10 MINUTES

COOKING TIME: 10 MINUTES

An eclectic mix of textures and flavours is involved in this smoothie. The end result is a fluffy pale green drink warmed with ginger and speckled with kiwi seeds. The lemon sorbet gives it a cooling effect making this ideal for a hot summer day.

kiwi fruit, ginger and lemon smoothie

SERVES 3

4 kiwi fruit, peeled and thickly sliced
150 ml/¼ pt/⅔ cup water, chilled

60 ml/4 tbsp ginger and lemon grass cordial
250 ml/8 fl oz/1 cup lemon sorbet

1 Blend all the ingredients until smooth.

2 Pour into glasses and drink straight away.

PREPARATION TIME: 5 MINUTES

This is a recipe that I have adapted from a smoothie that was made for me in a Cape Town juice bar. Cape Town loves its melon drinks so this recipe encompasses two: the deliciously sweet honeydew and the thirst-quenching watermelon.

mixed melon and ginger ale smoothie

SERVES 4

350 g/12 oz honeydew melon flesh, diced

450 g/1 lb watermelon flesh, diced
150 ml/¼ pt/⅔ cup dry ginger ale

1 Blend all the ingredients in two batches until smooth.

2 Pour into a bowl, then cover and chill for several hours.

3 Stir before serving in glasses.

PREPARATION TIME: 10 MINUTES

Sweet and exotic, this smoothie has an exquisite scent, instantly transporting the drinker to sunnier climes. Orange flower water is usually found in the baking sections of supermarkets and is essential in giving this smoothie its fragrant flavour.

melon and mango smoothie

SERVES 4

1 charentais or cantaloupe melon, halved and seeded (pitted)

600 ml/1 pt/2½ cups mango juice
30 ml/2 tbsp orange flower water

1 Scoop the melon flesh into the blender. Add the mango juice and orange flower water and blend until smooth.

2 Pour into a bowl, then cover and chill for several hours.

3 Stir before serving in glasses or mugs.

PREPARATION TIME: 7 MINUTES

One of the more adult smoothies in this section, this has a wonderful pink colour that can be quite a talking point. Campari can be bitter but this is softened by the sweetness of pineapple flesh combined with the sparkling red grape juice.

pineapple and sparkling campari smoothie

SERVES 3

450 g/1 lb pineapple flesh, cubed
300 ml/½ pt/1¼ cups sparkling red
   grape juice

30–60 ml/2–4 tbsp Campari

1   Place all the ingredients in the blender and blend until very smooth.

2   Strain to remove any fibrous pieces of pineapple remaining. Cover and chill.

3   Stir before serving in glasses or mugs.

PREPARATION TIME: 10 MINUTES

After a heavy meal, this is a refreshing drink. In this recipe it is best to use the white variant of crème de menthe so as not to discolour the beautiful yellow of the pineapple flesh. Try decorating the glasses with a small sprig of mint before serving.

minty fruit smoothie

SERVES 3

450 g/1 lb pineapple flesh, cubed
300 ml/½ pt/1¼ cups sparkling white
   grape juice

15–30 ml/1–2 tbsp crème de
   menthe

1   Place all the ingredients in the blender and blend until very smooth. Strain to remove any fibrous pieces of pineapple remaining. Cover and chill.

2   Stir before serving in glasses or mugs.

PREPARATION TIME: 10 MINUTES

Passion fruit has a highly aromatic pulp and its intense flavour makes it a popular addition to food and drink. With the variety of fruit included, this is a delicious and attractive pale golden smoothie, packed with crunchy passion fruit seeds.

fruit cocktail and passion fruit smoothie

SERVES 3–4

400 g/14 oz/1 large can of fruit cocktail
1 passion fruit, halved

300 ml/½ pt/1¼ cups passion fruit juice
45 ml/3 tbsp lemon juice

1 Tip the contents of the can of fruit cocktail into the blender. Scoop the passion fruit pulp and seeds directly over the fruit cocktail.

2 Add the passion fruit juice and lemon juice and blend until smooth.

3 Pour into a jug or bowl, cover and chill.

4 Stir before serving in glasses.

PREPARATION TIME: 7 MINUTES

Excellent as a breakfast smoothie and ideal for those who dislike the idea of eating something first thing in the morning. This is a cheerful, refreshing smoothie full of vitamin C. If you have the time, try using fresh ingredients rather than canned.

grapefruit, lime and lemon smoothie

SERVES 4

450 g/1 lb/1 very large can of
   grapefruit segments in juice or
   light syrup
Juice of 1 lime

Juice of 1 lemon
450 ml/¾ pt/2 cups fresh orange
   juice

1 Tip the contents of the can of grapefruit segments into the blender.

2 Add the three juices and blend until smooth. Cover and chill.

3 Stir before serving in glasses or mugs.

PREPARATION TIME: 10 MINUTES

A combination of delicious flavours makes this an enjoyable and nutritious smoothie. Grenadine is a blood-red, strong syrup made from pomegranates. It sweetens and provides a vibrant colour. This would make an excellent non-alcoholic drink.

pineapple and pear smoothie with grenadine

SERVES 4

410 g/14½ oz/1 large can of pears in juice
600 ml/1 pt/2½ cups pineapple juice

15 ml/1 tbsp grenadine syrup
Juice of 1 lemon

1 Tip the contents of the can of pears into the blender.

2 Add the remaining ingredients and blend until smooth. Cover and chill.

3 Stir before serving in glasses or mugs.

PREPARATION TIME: 5 MINUTES

A savoury smoothie that is similar to a tomato juice cocktail but with a kick. This is an easy recipe to adapt so try experimenting with different flavours. You could ring the changes by using turmeric or garam masala, for example.

curried tomato and mango chutney smoothie

SERVES 4

400 g/14 oz/1 large can of chopped tomatoes
300 ml/½ pt/1¼ cups water

45 ml/3 tbsp mango chutney
5 ml/1 tsp mild curry powder
25 g/1 oz coriander (cilantro) leaves

1   Tip the contents of the can of tomatoes into the blender.

2   Add the remaining ingredients and blend until smooth.

3   Pour into a bowl, then cover and chill for several hours.

4   Stir before serving in glasses or mugs

PREPARATION TIME: 5 MINUTES

mock bloody mary

SERVES 4

Prepare as for Curried Tomato and Mango Chutney Smoothie, but stir a shot of ice-cold vodka into each glass.

Using only the most refreshing ingredients, this smoothie is absolutely perfect for serving in warmer weather. It derives from an idea that was passed on to me by a Caribbean friend and can be either sweetened with sugar or serve salted.

caribbean cucumber and lime smoothie

SERVES 3–4

450 g/1 lb cucumber, peeled and
cut into chunks
Juice of 1 lime

450 ml/¾ pt/2 cups iced water
10–15 ml/2–3 tsp caster (superfine)
sugar

1 Place all the ingredients in the blender and blend until completely smooth.

2 Serve straight away in glasses.

PREPARATION TIME: 5 MINUTES

Another nutritious smoothie, packed with fibre and vitamins;
the combination of orange and beetroot (red beet) leads to a
sweet-sour flavour and a beautiful pink colour. Serve in tall
glasses packed with ice cubes for an unusual but healthy drink.

beetroot, orange and yoghurt smoothie

SERVES 4

350 g/12 oz sliced pickled beetroot
250 ml/8 fl oz/1 cup orange juice
300 ml/½ pt/1¼ cups water

A pinch of salt
150 ml/¼ pt/⅔ cup plain yoghurt

1 Blend all the ingredients in two batches in the blender.

2 Pour into a bowl, cover and chill.

3 Stir before serving in glasses or mugs

PREPARATION TIME: 5 MINUTES

INDEX